EXTRA INCOME
IN TIME OF
HARDSHIP

MARC-CHARLES NICOLAS

authorHOUSE®

AuthorHouse™
1663 Liberty Drive
Bloomington, IN 47403
www.authorhouse.com
Phone: 1 (800) 839-8640

Published by AuthorHouse 08/14/2018

ISBN: 978-1-5462-5565-9 (sc)
ISBN: 978-1-5462-5564-2 (e)

Library of Congress Control Number: 2018909660

Print information available on the last page.

CONTENTS

Preface xiii
About the Author.. xv
Introduction..xvii

Chapter 1 1
    1. Make Money From Your Own YouTube Channel................ 1
    2. Tips To Make Money From Your Own YouTube Channel .. 1
    3. Become An Affiliate Marketer 1
    4. Sell/Merchandise Products 2
    5. Utilize Fan Funding 2
    6. Become A YouTube Partner 2
Chapter 2 5
    1. Make Money From Flipping Houses................................. 5
    2. Evaluate The Neighborhood For Investment..................... 5
    3. Choose A House To Flip.. 6
    4. Gauge The Deal... 6
    5. Arrange Finances For Your Project.................................... 6
    6. Create Your Team To Move On.. 6
    7. Get Your House Ready For Sale 7
Chapter 3 8
    1. Make money from Affiliate Marketing.............................. 8
    2. How To Make Money From Affiliate Marketing 8
    3. Choose Your Affiliate Niche.. 9
    4. Choose An Affiliate Program 9

5. Set Up Your Blog 9

6. Disclose your Affiliate Relationship 9

7. Don't Forget Email Marketing 10

Chapter 4 11

1. Make Money Through Side Gigs – Get Paid Through
Airbnb, Lyft/Uber 11

2. Make Money Through Airbnb 11

3. Get Paid From Uber/Lyft 12

4. Make Money Online – Get Paid By Coaching And
Increase Your Online Reputation 12

5. Become A Private Coach 13

6. Start Group Coaching 13

7. Author A Book Or Start A DIY Program 13

8. Become An Affiliate Partner 14

Chapter 5 15

1. How To Make Money By Becoming A Freelancer 15

2. Making Money Online As A Freelancer 15

3. Start Data Mining 15

4. Use Your Writing Skills 16

5. Become A Graphic Designer 16

6. Become An Online Tutor 16

Chapter 6 17

1. What is Opt-in email method? 17

2. How to make money from Opt-in email marketing? 17

3. Example 18

Chapter 7 19

1. Various ways to get the Opt-in emails 19

2. Giving content for free 19

3. Gathering email address at checkout 19

4. Subscribe page 20

5. Next level: - Double Opt-in 20

Chapter 8 21

1. Make money with Google AdSense account 21

2. How to apply for Google AdSense program? 21

3. Revenue 22

4. Tips and tricks for approval 22

Chapter 9 23

   1. How to make money from Google Adwords?.................... 23

   2. What Google Says about Adwords.................................. 23

   3. Best way to make money from Google Adwords.............. 24

   4. Create a Google Adwords account 24

   5. Pick a Keyword and start promoting............................. 24

Chapter 10 26

   1. How to make money from 3D printing? 26

   2. Make money with a 3D printer 26

   3. Print for Tech 27

   4. Create online courses or videos 27

   5. Make money without a 3D printer................................ 27

Chapter 11 28

   1. Surviving a Recession... 28

   2. Stay in touch with your support systems: 28

   3. Re-establish a workable routine.................................... 29

   4. Stay in touch with previous contacts: 29

   5. Draw up a revised budget: 29

   6. Don't forget to still have fun: 30

   7. Remain active in the community: 30

   8. Retain a positive attitude: 30

   9. Remember that there is a world of opportunity out there... 31

Chapter 12 32

   A selection of Options for making extra money 32

   1. Caring for Companion Animals 32

   What can you expect to be doing in general if you take
care of a pet for someone? 32

      • Feeding and watering 32

      • Cleaning up 33

      • Exercising 33

      • Grooming... 33

      • Visits to the vet.. 33

   Dogs: 33

   Cats and other pets: 34

   2. House sitting 35

   Making extra money through your hobby.............................. 35

- CONDUCT A MARKET AND COMPETITIVE ANALYSIS 35
- DESIGN A MARKETING PLAN 35
- SOURCE A MENTOR 36
- GUARD AGAINST BURNOUT 36
- BECOME PROFESSIONAL 36

Art, craft and hobby options. 36

    PAINTING 37

    ART POTTERY 37

- ANTIQUE ART POTTERY 38

Chapter 13 40

Ongoing Options 40

Making money as a handy man. 40

Beginning a landscaping business from home. 42

Making money as a babysitter 44

Making money as a fish keeping consultant 45

    PAYING FOR PARKING 47

    BANKING FEES 47

    WARRANTIES 47

    GENERAL INVESTING ADVICE 48

    CREDIT REPORTS 48

    ONLINE SHOPPING 48

    RENTAL VEHICLE INSURANCE 48

    STUDENT AID 48

Chapter 14 49

Starting an internet business 49

Using the internet to beat tough times. 49

Don't be too concerned about a financial outlay. 49

    AFFILIATE MARKETING 50

    AFFILIATE PROGRAMS 50

    SEARCH ENGINE OPTIMIZATION (SEO) 50

Domain name: 51

    INDEXING YOUR WEBSITE 51

    HOSTING YOUR WEBSITE 52

    E-MAIL MARKETING 52

- SET UP AN AUTOMATIC E-MAIL RESPONDER 52
- DON'T EVER SPAM 53

- Be aware of your wording 53
- Source the correct auto responder software...... 53
  Dream Boards 53
Chapter 15 55
  NON-WEBSITE ventures..................................... 55
    Money from forums 55
    - Making money as a Freelancer 56
    - Create an account....................................... 57
  Writing an E-Book: 57
    E-Books 57
Chapter 16 59
  Working smart 59
  Design your business around your passions and interests 59
    Remember to always get the basics right.......................... 59
  Invest in your new business................................... 60
  Do not be discouraged by negative people. 60
Chapter 17 62
  Back to pets and how to earn big money from small fishes 62
    People and pets 62
    A pet for all occasions.................................... 63
    The problems associated with wild caught fish................. 63
    The secrets of breeding fish for money 63
    Choosing which species to breed 63
    - Discus 64
    - Oscars 64
    - Piranhas 65
    Spawning tanks... 65
    Additional equipment 65
    Diet for your adult fish 66
    Show me the money 66
Chapter 18 67
  Growing and selling vegetables............................... 67
    Source you compost 67
    Designate an area for your vegetable garden 67
    Prepare your vegetable beds............................... 67
    Plant your seedlings 68

Caring for your seeds 68

Harvesting your vegetables 68

Be an environmentally friendly gardener 68

- Soapy water 68

- Tobacco spray 69

- Garlic and onion spray 69

An indoor vegetable garden 69

Chapter 19 70

Domestic services 70

Washing and ironing 70

Cleaning homes 71

Chapter 20 72

"I really want your business" 72

Offer your clients something for free 72

Outstanding service 72

Reduced fees 73

Buy one get one free 73

Samples 73

Develop your people skills 73

Be completely honest 73

Insist on a contract 73

Stick to the time line 74

Look the part 74

Be courteous and polite 75

Chapter 21 76

Additional tips on saving 76

Check your change 76

Holiday in a friend's home 76

Vehicle purchases 77

Make an effort to save 77

Continue your payments 77

Credit cards 77

Tax 78

Understand the potential problems of a "dual earning
family" 78

- Domestic help 78
- Child care 78
- Labor – saving luxuries 78
- Transport costs.. 79
- Double wardrobes 79
- Taxation.. 79
Chapter 22 80
  Develop the correct mind set 80
    Develop a winning attitude 81
- Change your reality...................................... 81
- Choose to be wealthy 82
- Do not be put off by your own perceptions 82

PREFACE

During difficult financial periods, your boss no longer cares if you are hard working, smart, diligent and dedicated. The onset of a recession invariably means that many people are going to be laid off.

People may also loose their jobs through unfair layoffs, either because the company is no longer prospering or has been sold off.

Fortunately, the fact that you are not working for a boss or company, does not have to mean the end of the road for anyone. Today, more than ever before, ordinary people can make a good living, working for themselves.

Extra Income in Time of hardship, written by Marc-Charles Nicolas will vigorously and eloquently explain the many varied means of making a living in time of hardship, during a recession, layoff or any other difficult financial time. This fine book is a synopsis of Marc-Charles' experience running e-commerce, community website, selling and investing in different avenues.

ABOUT THE AUTHOR

Marc-Charles is a professional system administrator, a software architect, a published author and an upcoming Real Estate investor who holds a bachelor's degree in Agri-Business Engineering. He pursued his interest in computers at Oklahoma City University where he graduated with an M.B.A. in Management of Information System. After graduation, he found work at IBM as a programming languages software engineer, then a UNIX commands Software Engineer and later a Kernel Software Engineer.

His profile ranks, among the most technically diverse and knowledgeable computer or information technology professionals. With over 20 years of business and IT experience, he has built his career in the highly competitive world of Information technology. He has worked for some of the largest technological and financial corporations of the world such as IBM, Hewlett Packard, Dell / Perot Systems, Siemens, Alcon Labs, Bank of America, Citi Group, JP Morgan Chase, Washington Mutual, etc.

He is someone who sees it as his goal to raise the current level of thinking and pragmatism around him.

An entrepreneur at heart, fueled by his dreams and inimitable drive, he is no stranger to online entrepreneurship. He has put his time and effort into creating online income from different types of websites and even from eBay. As a webmaster, Owner and creator of different websites, Marc-Charles has learned many ways to monetize his website traffic using advertising third-party products or services on the websites. He has used AdSense AdWords, Facebook ads for instance to make extra income off the web.

In this book, he is sharing the very practical and genuine ways to earn extra income in totally legal ways.

This book is not about how to get rich, but how to enjoy monthly passive income. It is not about how to change the bulk of your income, but it is a list of passive, semi- passive and active income ideas put together.

INTRODUCTION

"Extra Income in Time of Recession" has been written to highlight the numerous options available to the person who is:

- Facing layoff because of a recession or a retrenchment (work reduction).
- Interested in supplementing their existing income during a recession.
- Leaving their nine to five careers to begin a "work from home" business.

It may surprise you to know that there are a great many opportunities for a person to make an income during difficult financial times.

This is the age of the internet and a number of these opportunities are related to affiliate marketing and related activities on the "world wide web", which include:

- Affiliate Marketing
- Search engine optimization (SEO)
- Website creation
- Niche development
- Online advertising
- Real Estate
- Insurance

When approached correctly, affiliate marketing and related activities will allow a person to create multiple income streams and you will still be able to earn money even without having a product to sell and without requiring customer support. Once you begin to build up your own internet business, you will be able to generate money passively in part, that is to say: while you are busy with a hobby or sport or out with the family, your business will be generating money on your behalf.

Other work from home possibilities include: selling items, which may again be through the internet (eBay / Craigslist), or selling items using apps such as: 5miles and LetGo and OfferUp, etc. It could also be through local newspaper or with flyers.

If you are creative and have a flair for designing, painting, pottery, sculpture (and the list goes on) you can make various items that can be sold at craft fairs or at similar outlets.

Everyone has unique talents and whether on a part time or full-time basis, people can repair vehicles; perform various domestic "maintenance" type jobs such as painting, woodwork, swimming pool maintenance and general garden upkeep.

Working from home, either through choice or because you have been laid off, offers many benefits, but the greatest benefit is that you will no longer be "trading time for money". People with full time jobs, may earn a little or a great deal, but as soon as they stop working, they stop earning money immediately. Certain work from home opportunities, such as internet marketing, allows you to generate money passively once you have done the initial ground work. If you can establish a successful work from home business, you will never have to fear being laid off again.

One of the greatest moves I have made, I have learned how to flip houses and learn more about purchasing a property at a low cost and do the repairs and resale. Flipping houses can be an amazing business if you are willing to make the steps and learn. The profit can really be unbelievable and to me Real Estate is one of the best ways to become "your own boss"

A home business is not for everyone though. Many people have become "institutionalized". They have worked for a boss for so long that they do not believe that they can run their own business. Many people do not have the will power to dedicate the time required for home business success, but for those of you who are ready to begin, this book will offer many examples of how to earn additional income and will guide you through the many steps required to become successful.

CHAPTER 1

1. Make Money From Your Own YouTube Channel

While thinking of YouTube as a mere video hosting platform, did you ever wonder why does every other video channel ask you to subscribe? Well, YouTube bears tremendous potential for bloggers and video creators to make money. As a YouTube creator, you not only popularize yourself among the masses, or gain readership, or help the community, but you also earn a lot if everything goes right. For the people looking for options to make money online, YouTube serves as a wonderful platform.

2. Tips To Make Money From Your Own YouTube Channel

If you are a YouTuber or are planning to join this platform, then this book is for you. Here we list some of the top ways to make money from your own YouTube channel.

3. Become An Affiliate Marketer

Affiliate marketing forms a crucial part of online advertising strategies. You can not only use this strategy for blogs but can also monetize your YouTube channel by becoming an affiliate. You just must showcase sponsored contents in your videos. You are not required to brag about the brands. Rather simple and fact-based promotion of the brands would suffice.

Affiliate marketing is becoming popular among the brands since there are no risks. However, as the brand would only pay you when you generate sales for them, you may probably find it a bit tough to make money fast through this method.

4. Sell/Merchandise Products

YouTube provides a great platform for selling products. You can easily create engaging videos displaying your products, or you can show sponsored products as well to make money. People like to view such videos as they get significant information from a single video without hassle. Small items such as T-shirts, mugs, and stationery, etc., work best for such videos.

5. Utilize Fan Funding

'Fan funding' on YouTube is somewhat similar to crowdfunding. If you generate engaging content in your videos, your audience would be happy to support your channel through donations as they want you to continue providing them such useful information through your videos.

You really need to know not just about Paypal, but also about tools such as Patreon. A lot of people are now using Patreon to accept donation. Patreon is a membership platform that provides business tools for creators to run a subscription content service, as well as ways for artists to build relationships and provide exclusive experiences to their subscribers, or "patrons.

6. Become A YouTube Partner

Becoming a YouTube partner will open new horizons for YouTube monetization to you. YouTube is a great educational tool with more than 100 hours of content videos uploaded every minute. It is watched by hundreds of millions of people all over the globe. Just verify your account through the Creator Studio section to allow monetization. You can now apply Google Adsense to your channel to generate revenue from ads. Sign in to your Adsense account and adjust the advertising network settings. You will now see a '$' symbol with your videos showing that your videos are all set to make money. Keep in mind that by just having a lot of people subscribed to your YouTube channel doesn't guarantee that you will make a lot of money. YouTube does not pay that much per videos viewed, but it really depends on the quality of the video, the topic. Really, you must be a top influencer to make big money on YouTube. According to Emon I., you could conclude that 100,000 subscribers are worth $1,600, so 1 subscriber is worth $0.016 . If you want to make money with your videos on YouTube, you must learn the "Rules for monetization on YouTube". Learn how to drive people to your website, your ecommerce or whatever website where you are selling products or ads.

You must decide to know who you are or who you want to be on YouTube. Do you want to be a micro-influencer, a macro influencer or a mega-influencer? As you can see in the graph below a micro-influencer, influences between 1000 to 25000 people. A macro-influencer or mid-tier influencer reaches between 25000 to 100,000 people and from 100000 people to millions of people you become a celebrity or a mega-influencer.

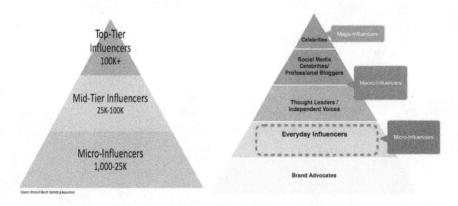

YouTube is not just an infotainment platform, rather, it also serves as an incredible marketplace allowing people to make money.

If you plan to make money from ads, you must know the types of ads. It is good to review terms like CPC or CPV, In-Search, in display and pre-roll. According to Masud Karim in his article how to make $2000 a month https://www.quora.com/How-many-YouTube-subscribers-do-I-need-to-make-2000-a-month

Cost Per Click (CPC)

CPC is when an advertiser pays money based on clicks. So, if a certain keyword has a CPC of $3 and someone clicks on that ad, it will charge that advertiser $3.

Cost Per View (CPV)

CPV is when an advertiser pays money based on views. A view for the advertiser means someone watches an Ad for at least 30 seconds or half of the ad; whichever comes first. That person could click that ad 50 times but it still wouldn't charge the advertiser more because they're not paying for the click, they're paying for the view.

TrueView: Pre-Roll, In-Search & In-Display Ads

Pre-Roll Ads are the ads that act as a preview before the video starts and viewers can skip it after 5 seconds.

In-Search Ads show up in the search results and are surrounded by a light yellow box.

In-Display Ads show up on the right side of YouTube in the suggested video

You just must go right with your videos. With the tips mentioned above, we are positive that you will enjoy monetizing your YouTube channel. Good luck!

CHAPTER 2

1. Make Money From Flipping Houses

Flipping houses is getting more attention these days as it seems an easy approach to make money. However, those who practically step into this niche know well how difficult it is to make money from flipping houses. Yet, as the saying goes 'nothing is impossible', making money from this method isn't impossible too. You just must learn the basic stepwise procedure to reach your goal.

In this book, we will guide you on how to generate money from house flipping.

2. Evaluate The Neighborhood For Investment

In the first step, you must decide on a neighborhood to begin with house flipping. You cannot just start your work in any other locality. Rather, you must know the market rates for the houses in a neighborhood, the profitability of that area, and the potential to increase the prices in future. You must keep a keen eye on the newspapers, blogs, and other resources to stay aware of the market trends. It is good to visit realtors. com and Zillow.com, etc. to check on the new listed houses and on the price, they are being sold for. Remember you are looking for potential and bargain.

3. Choose A House To Flip

After finalizing a neighborhood, you now must choose a house to flip. Although, there are no set rules to make the right selection. Nonetheless, you can check the potential in a house through referrals, personal visits, MLS, and advertisements. You can also get in touch with brokers and contractors who are looking for someone to assist their business for a small fee.

4. Gauge The Deal

After you decide on the neighborhood and the house, you now must evaluate the profitability of the deal. Your goal to flip houses is to make money through profitable flipping. Hence, you must analyze the ARV (after repair value) for the house since you will be selling the house after investing some money for repairs and maintenance. Most successful flippers employ the 70% rule for ARV.

5. Arrange Finances For Your Project

Flipping houses first require a little investment from you. For this, you must arrange for finance. Some of the best options for lending money include the Hard Money Lenders, Private Money Lenders, Bank Loans, and Real Estate Crowdfunding Loans. Communicate with them as openly as you can to convince them for lending money to you. You need to know about foundation work on a house. The inspectors do not want the slope to be more than one point. From 0.1 to 0.9 point is acceptable when it comes to the foundation of a house.

6. Create Your Team To Move On

Now that you have the finance with you, the next step is to gather your team to work on your dream project. In fact, you can also develop good relationships with the contractors, appraisers, inspectors, and lawyers to assist you later in your fix and flip career.

7. GET YOUR HOUSE READY FOR SALE

Now that you have your team, you just must get your house ready for a profitable sale. Let your contractors work for you, ensure timely completion of every step, and charm a buyer to purchase the house. Make sure to sell the house as quickly as possible to lower down the carrying costs.

Flipping houses can be a lucrative career for those who want to build lasting relationships in the market. You just must be keen on analyzing the market trends to make the right deal at the right time.

CHAPTER 3

1. MAKE MONEY FROM AFFILIATE MARKETING

Whenever you search for ways to make money while sitting at home, you will eventually stumble upon the option of 'affiliate marketing'. Most tech gurus suggest affiliate marketing as a key method to generate huge revenue from blogging. However, some of the new affiliate marketers often fail at making money at the very beginning, so they think of it as an unviable option. Nonetheless, this isn't the case. If you go in the right direction from the start, you will eventually see tremendous profitability in this niche.

2. HOW TO MAKE MONEY FROM AFFILIATE MARKETING

A lucrative benefit behind affiliate marketing is that it requires no investment from you. You just must own a platform for grabbing the audience, such a blog or a YouTube channel. The rest will be done by your affiliate brand.

Here is how you should proceed to make money from affiliate marketing.

3. CHOOSE YOUR AFFILIATE NICHE

If you are a blogger, you must have an idea about the preferences of your readers. So, you can choose an affiliate from the niche of your readers. If you are a newcomer in the field, you can select any good affiliate and generate your blog around it by delivering quality and informative content to grab more readers. The same applies to YouTubers as well.

4. CHOOSE AN AFFILIATE PROGRAM

Now that you have decided on a niche, the next step is to decide about the affiliate program. These days, Amazon affiliate marketing is becoming increasingly popular. Amazon offers incredible rates to the affiliate marketers. In Addition, owing to its diversity, the marketplace sufficiently caters many marketers from various niches. It is always likely that your chosen niche would also be present on Amazon, whether it is about technology or lifestyle.

Likewise, you can also choose from WordPress affiliate marketing programs, such as Freelancer, SiteGround, WP Engine, Studio Press, MaxCDN, and a lot more.

5. SET UP YOUR BLOG

The key to successful affiliate marketing is creativity. Whether you choose blogging, YouTube channel, or any other method of marketing, you must always make sure to create engaging content to attract readership. After you decide about the affiliate marketing niche and program, you now must decide about the content (whether blogs, videos, or eCourse) to grab the audience.

6. DISCLOSE YOUR AFFILIATE RELATIONSHIP

It is always good to win the trust of your readers by disclosing your affiliate relationship. They would be happy to know about your status and would trust your content. Plus, this is also a requirement by FTC's endorsement rules to disclose about it.

7. Don't Forget Email Marketing

While your content would suffice to gain readers, you cannot deny the importance of email lists for personalized marketing. Make sure you use this technique alongside your regular content to redirect readers to the website.

Affiliate marketing can bring a great deal of profitability with it. However, before jumping into this niche, make sure you gain sufficient knowledge to make your hard work pay off. Otherwise, all your efforts will go in vain.

CHAPTER 4

1. Make Money Through Side Gigs – Get Paid Through Airbnb, Lyft/Uber

Thanks to the rise in technology, that people are now offered a plethora of options to work on a part-time basis. In fact, some of the services that were previously limited to full-time jobs are now also offered as a side gig, for instance, to become a driver. The reason why side gigs are becoming popular is that people cannot earn a sufficient amount through single full-time jobs to meet their needs. Besides, they cannot manage a second job either since they must maintain the work-life balance as well.

Side gigs allow you to work as per your convenience. Whenever you have some leisure time, you can opt for one or the other side gig to make extra money. When you are running short of time, you can take a break.

We have been hearing a lot about Uber, Lyft, and Airbnb these days for generating extra money. Are they productive? Read long to find out how you can exploit these services as side gigs.

2. Make Money Through Airbnb

Airbnb is a cloud-based house rental service bridging the gap between the house owners and the customers looking for some premises on rent. For those who own big houses, have extra rooms in their homes, or want to rent their apartments for a short-term, Airbnb provides a wonderful platform.

If you have some extra space in your house that you want to share with a guest, you can become an Airbnb host. The procedure is quite easy – you can register yourself on the website for free and create a listing to get attention. You can either create a listing for shared rooms, private rooms, or the entire premises, depending upon the availability of space.

Once done, you can get your account verified by uploading appropriate photos of yourself as well as of your premises. A verified account gains trust from the customers. You are now ready to start making money from Airbnb.

Airbnb charges 3% service fee for hosts. It means you still have a large amount left with you as your earning. As an Airbnb host, you can easily earn around $924 (average) monthly.

3. Get Paid From Uber/Lyft

Earlier, becoming a driver was a full-time and a tiring job with very low wages. However, thanks to the online taxi services such as Uber and Lyft, people can now earn sufficient money by using their driving skills. These services are always looking for licensed drivers to cater to the requirements of their customers. The reason why they are becoming so popular today is that you are not a contractual employee of Uber or Lyft. Nor you must formally resign from your services if you need a break. You can simply choose to work as per your schedule to earn extra money. All you need to have is a good driving experience, a valid driving license, and a car. You can swiftly earn from $364 to $377 on an average by joining Uber and Lyft respectively as a driver.

4. Make Money Online – Get Paid By Coaching And Increase Your Online Reputation

While you are looking for ways to make extra money from home, why not leverage your skills for that? Many people around you would be lagging in various skills or simply lack the motivation to step ahead in their lives. In other words, they need a "coach"! If you have a good online reputation, adequate knowledge, teaching skills, and convincing power then you can leverage all these traits to become an online coach.

Coaching or online consultation is becoming increasingly popular for making extra money. You don't necessarily have to be a subject specialist to become a coach. Rather you can simply begin online consultations and lifestyle coaching to motivate the people around you.

Here we list some of the best ways to make money through coaching.

5. Become A Private Coach

Private coaching is the most common way of online coaching. In this niche, you simply have a one-on-one interaction with your clients looking for consultation, such as business consultancy. The biggest plus with this sort of coaching is that you don't have to invest anything before taking a start. Nor do you need to own an office. Even a simple Skype or phone call would suffice to begin with your online coaching career. You can easily earn anywhere between $100 and $400 an hour through this job.

6. Start Group Coaching

Group coaching is a popular business model that has been around for quite a few years. As a group coach, you directly interact with people to solve their problems. You can either begin as a group coach by setting up physical workplace, or you can arrange online interactive sessions through various portals, and live/recorded webinars.

7. Author A Book Or Start A DIY Program

Another way to utilize your knowledge and skills to make money is to become an author or start a DIY program for your clients. Either way, you get a wonderful opportunity to interact with your clients passively. Although this method is a bit slow to make money and requires a lot of enthusiasm and efforts from your end, you won't mind waiting for a while before you begin enjoying fruitful results. Not only this method helps you make money but also earns you a good reputation.

8. Become An Affiliate Partner

Becoming an affiliate not only works best for marketing purposes, but also helps you start as an online coach. You can interact with other successful coaches having similar demographics to attract their audience by becoming a referral or affiliate partner. It does not mean you are poaching, rather you are simply providing more information to the visitors through your referral program.

When compared to the other methods to make money online, coaching may not seem as quick as others. However, with a little patience, you can eventually become a successful online coach who not only earns good money but also enjoys a credible reputation among the readers.

CHAPTER 5

1. How To Make Money By Becoming A Freelancer

Gone are the days when freelancing was merely a side gig. Today, you can earn more than your full-time job as a freelancer. All you must do is to opt the right niche for freelancing that matches your skills.

2. Making Money Online As A Freelancer

When you initially decide to become a freelancer, you may wonder what special you can do to outshine your profile in a marketplace flooded with freelancers. To ease your stress, here we list the top ways through which you can earn nicely as a freelancer.

3. Start Data Mining

Data mining is one of the easiest ways to make money online. Owing to the time taking nature of the work, many companies look for freelancers to help them. Although, in the beginning, you may not get good gigs. However, with a little patience, you can develop your profile as a pro data miner with a keen eye on minute details. Considering the demand for this profession, it is a safe bet to say that data mining is among those never-ending jobs that always pay off.

4. Use Your Writing Skills

Writing is a skill that has always been in demand since ancient times. And, speculatively, this skill will continue to gain attention till the end of time. Thanks to the technology, that people can now leverage their writing skills to make money easy while sitting at home. You just must have good writing skills, in-depth knowledge of various subjects, a computer and internet connection. As a freelance writer, you have a plethora of options to write. Maybe you suffer a bit in the beginning, yet, after a while, you will be generating huge earnings through this single skill.

5. Become A Graphic Designer

If you have a creative mind, then graphic designing is a wonderful niche to become a pro freelancer. Just like writing, graphic designing brings with it endless opportunities to earn money. From website layouts to icons and logos, to magazine covers, ads, banners, and infographics, you are offered a wide range of high paying jobs even from the beginning. You just must excel using designing software and tools to come up with the most accurate designs as needed by the clients.

6. Become An Online Tutor

If you are a subject specialist, have an internet connection, and a passion for teaching, you can certainly become an online tutor. To become a freelance online tutor, you neither must spend hours and hours on creating an article, nor you must excel using any software. With a little effort, you can earn huge amounts through online tutoring.

Becoming a freelancer is a safe way to earn money, to say goodbye to your previous job and to become your own boss. Initially, you may have to struggle a bit to establish your online presence. But, once done, you will enjoy working according to your own preferences and earning as much as you want.

CHAPTER 6

1. What is Opt-in email method?

Opt-in email strategy for building an email list falls under the realm of email marketing. Opt-in email method of marketing is when the consumers have already registered or opted to receive further information or promotional material via emails. But unlike bulk emailing or spamming, opt-in email list building is a sure way of getting conversions as the user shows the willingness to try the product or service being offered by submitting their email address. Once the email addresses are registered or captured promotional emails can be sent to these addresses through bulk email sending software or web platforms.

2. How to make money from Opt-in email marketing?

One of the best online marketing approaches is to offer some reward like free eBook or option to register for online seminars related to a niche by encouraging the users to register their email. Once the email is captured, it can be used to promote any product and make sales within the niche or related to one.

3. EXAMPLE

A website promoting adventure gear can have a single page which provides a free eBook on camping upon registering the email. The email list built through this method can act as a source of revenue whenever targeted with good promotional emails. Every time an email is sent to all opt-in subscribers, the chance of making sales is high. Sometimes it can act as an autopilot too. You can use any web tool to plan your first email to your last for each new user. Targeting and retargeting through emails will end up in sales and without much effort and with pre-written emails cash flow is possible.

Note: - Always allow your users to unsubscribe from your email list whenever they deem it necessary else you will fall into spamming category and will impact your reputation and promotional capabilities.

CHAPTER 7

1. Various ways to get the Opt-in emails

Offer coupon code or discount

The best way to encourage the customer is to offer some discount on the price or offer code for their email subscription. There are several third-party websites that only attract users who are looking for any discount or coupon codes for various products.

2. Giving content for free

A single sign up page can be built into your website that allows the visitors to download free educational content like an eBook upon entering their email address.

3. Gathering email address at checkout

Making sales is the goal of any marketing strategy, right?

But why stop at that one sale, why not lure the customer into more sales by thanking them and asking their email address after they check out.

4. SUBSCRIBE PAGE

Blogs can have a pop up subscribe form for the related topics. Readers can opt for your blog updates and new blogs regarding the same niche. Whenever you create a new blog your subscribers will get an email through an automated process, and this will be your instant traffic source, and traffic equals money.

5. NEXT LEVEL: - DOUBLE OPT-IN

Double Opt-in method not only gathers the email address but confirms the subscription by sending an email for activation.

Opt-in email has raised the benchmark for email marketing by proving itself more effective and sure method of high conversion rates by targeting people who desired the service or product offered by the subscription, by registering their email address.

CHAPTER 8

1. Make money with Google AdSense account

Google AdSense is an advertisement program that allows website owners or YouTubers to earn money by displaying ads with their content. The program is free to join, and anyone regardless of their country or content type (exception: betting, gambling, and adult content) can apply and start earning money whenever a user clicks on the ads.

2. How to apply for Google AdSense program?

To apply for Google AdSense, one should either have a website or a YouTube channel with some content already attracting the users. Start by creating a good-looking rich content website or create a great YouTube channel with content you want to promote. After that apply online, fill up all the necessary details in the application page and get verified. After a few days, you will receive an email stating the acceptance or rejection of your application. Once the application is accepted, you get temporary access to the AdSense account which allows you to place ads and lets you check your revenue stats. All the details regarding the placement of the ads are simplified so that no technical knowledge about development is required. Keep in mind that you have temporary access till now, you can generate revenue by clicks, but you cannot withdraw you're earning yet. To get the payments, you need to go through a second verification process which includes your PIN (Sent by Google at your address), Bank account and tax information to be verified.

3. REVENUE

Once you have done all the formalities and have an active AdSense account you will start to make money according to your traffic. You will get paid through the mode chosen by you either by wire transfers or through checks. Payments are only made from your AdSense account once it reaches a limit of $100.

4. TIPS AND TRICKS FOR APPROVAL

Google AdSense is the best program for the publishers the rates are the highest in the market. Therefore, the approval rate is also low. Not all the applications get approved, only the ones with good quality content and meeting the requirements get to see the approvals. Apart from quality content, there are few things beginners can consider before applying to increase the chance of getting in. The biggest mistake person applying for the first time do is, they apply without having a proper website. Any website should be properly created with policy page, about us page and contact page, all present in the header or footer of your website.

There is no limit to the revenue generation through AdSense. As a publisher, you will get to know about google ads more and more, and you can plan accordingly for content creation. Just don't click your own ads, Google will detect it and may ban your account.

CHAPTER 9

1. How to make money from Google Adwords?

Google AdWords is the biggest online advertising platform. It is target based auction system for advertisements, where Advertisers compete for the ad space on the search engine results. If you have familiarity with Google AdSense already or you are a publisher monetizing your content with AdSense, then you know Google Adwords is the platform where the bids are placed to get advertising space. Yes, people bid to get space on your website or YouTube channel to show their ads, and that's Google Adwords.

Simply put, AdSense is for the publishers, and Adwords is for the advertisers.

2. What Google Says about Adwords

According to Google their majority of revenue is coming from the advertisers using Adwords. As more and more manufacturers and service providers are feeling the need for the online presence, online advertising is a multi-Billion dollar industry.

3. BEST WAY TO MAKE MONEY FROM GOOGLE ADWORDS

There are numerous ways in which you can earn money from Adwords, unlike AdSense in some cases you don't even need your own website. You can simply become a member of any affiliate program and start your advertising campaign using Adwords and make money through the affiliate payment systems.

For success in Adwords, you need to understand the affiliate marketing and the product parameters you are promoting. The chances of success become high if you have a great product and a very good affiliate program to motivate you to post ads on Google.

Take these steps and start your Adwords; money making machine
Become a member of an affiliate program

Choose from thousands of affiliate programs and a niche to promote; this is the first step and a very crucial one as well. You will be paying Google through your Adwords account by bidding for ad space. Therefore, your affiliate program should be a high paying one, and your niche should be the one in demand but with less competition. Google AdWords keyword planner tool will help you to find a killing product for your campaign, and you can check the ad rates as well.

Some of the popular high paying Affiliate Networks are: Clickbank, Cj affiliate, ShareAsale, and Amazon.

4. CREATE A GOOGLE ADWORDS ACCOUNT

Use your Gmail account to create Adwords account for free. You can provide the URL of your website if you have one or any URL will do, you can also use your affiliate marketing website URL.

5. PICK A KEYWORD AND START PROMOTING

After the login, you can create an ad campaign and start promoting your URL or page link to which you want the traffic to be directed.

Choose the demographic well as this will impact the bidding price and your overall ad campaign. You can choose your keywords related to your product or service having less competition and high search volume, this way you pay less for each click. Your ad will appear in the first 2 or 3 spots of search results in Google. From there on everything is on autopilot. People searching on Google will see your ad if it's relevant to their search they will click on it reaches the landing page and if they like your offer, it will be converted in to a sale and you will get a commission through your affiliate website.

Both Google AdSense and Adwords can prove to be a money-making machine, but both are different. Adwords need you to invest in your ad campaigns to drive traffic and make sales. One cannot argue about the level of significance of both.

CHAPTER 10

1. How to make money from 3D printing?

3D printing is not the thing of future anymore it's real, and it's here. Still, it's relatively new technology but people are using it to create 3D prints through brilliant designs and are pioneers.

With cost being near as of a high-end laser printer anyone can own one and find various ways to monetize the use of a 3D printer. There are ways in which you don't even need a printer you can sell your designs and 3D prints.

From designing to making a 3D printout, you can be anywhere in this process and still make money. The makerspace community in Dallas-Fort Worth, mainly the Carrollton, TX makerspace branch offers its members the possibility to use 3D printers. Members can be found 3D printing, recording podcasts in the AV room, or developing independent video games or creating items. Certain members get to sell their 3D printing online for example.

2. Make money with a 3D printer

Print and Sell

Start printing the designs you think can be viral or let the customers choose for themselves through your online store. Online store building platforms like Shopify will let you build your own store for free. Print your

26

designs or the ones you bought and add them to your store. This method works if you have a 3D printer and you are helping the buyers by removing the trouble to get a 3D printer.

3. Print for Tech

Many tech firms and miniature model companies require prototypes printed. You can write an email to them indicating your skill in the field and specs of your 3D printer and your experience with it. Get a contract for the long run and deliver on time and make money.

Platforms like 3Dhub will allow you to register with them as a 3D printer owner and get local printing work. Animators, Jewelers, and designers all require 3D printing to analyze their work in detail; all potential customers either online or on a local level.

4. Create online courses or videos

3D printing is still a new area for designing and digital arts. You can create your own course and turn it into an eBook or a YouTube video and create a niche of your own. 3D printing videos alone with time-lapse make tons of money with YouTube channels.

5. Make money without a 3D printer

Designing

You can go online and find the portals like Shapeways to post the designs for 3D printing by creating your own online store of 3D objects. You can sell your designs or make custom ones as per the requirement of 3D printing companies. Or you can find a person with a printer and collaborate to make cool models and sell them.

CHAPTER 11

1. Surviving a Recession

Recessions represent a slowdown of economic activity and a wide spread decline in trade and employment opportunities over an (invariably extended) period, which may last up to a year, if not more.

At a point, the government (normally) intervenes by decreasing taxation and increasing money supply, but there several very important steps that you can take, particularly if you are facing layoff, to survive the recession.

The most difficult element to accept is when you are personally targeted through layoff.

Before you can begin to earn income again through full time employment (if that is what you choose), you need to survive the process of layoff and the following guidelines will be helpful:

2. Stay in touch with your support systems:

- Most people have family or friends who they can look to in times of need. Forced layoff or time of shortage is nothing to be ashamed about. It comes about because of decisions that are beyond your control and the opportunity to talk to people who you trust, is important for your emotional well being. Many highly qualified people of sound mind, experience depression to various degrees after facing layoff and it is vital to these folks have a support system that keeps them level headed. Friends and family may also be able to assist you to find employment once again.

3. RE-ESTABLISH A WORKABLE ROUTINE

The thought of being able to sleep late appeals to most folk and may be one of the activities you previously looked forward to on your day/s off or when you were on vacation, but not getting up at a reasonable time once you have been retrenched or laid off, is counter productive. This is because you will need a solid routine during the period that you are not working. The lack of routine invariably leads to a downward spiral and the sense of uselessness. The first hugely important thing that you need to do immediately after facing layoff is to draw up a realistic schedule and follow it to the letter.

4. STAY IN TOUCH WITH PREVIOUS CONTACTS:

- People who are working will be in a better position than you are to hear about job offers and it makes sense to utilize these people's knowledge. Wherever feasible, try to meet with many of these people from time to time, even if it is only over a cup of coffee.

5. DRAW UP A REVISED BUDGET:

- The period during which you are not working, may be short or (very) long, so it is important to completely review your budget. Become familiar with both your "static" and "non-static" items on your budget. Home mortgage or rent, utility bills and loans represent static expenses, which are also the more difficult to cut down on due to their nature. You may, in effect, not be able to cut back on any of these at all. Non-static items include groceries, clothing, entertainment and the like. Many of these items may be pure luxury and it is here that the most severe budget cuts will need to take place. Pure luxury expenses, of necessity, must be lost, even if doing so requires that you need to clean your own swimming pool or iron your own laundry. This is also the time to consider destroying your credit cards. Cutting one, more or all your credit cards, although frightening, is often the first concrete step to regain control of your finances.

6. DON'T FORGET TO STILL HAVE FUN:

- Layoff or retrenchment does not have to be the darkest period in your life. In fact, to prevent depression, you should be getting involved with fun activities wherever possible (provided these are not causing you to go over budget).

7. REMAIN ACTIVE IN THE COMMUNITY:

This will invariably involve volunteering your time and services if possible. But this needs not be a negative thing. To some degree you will be rubbing shoulders with people who do still have jobs and you may be noticed by someone who is in the position to re-employ you. Volunteering also helps ward off depression as the activities you will be involved with, give purpose to your day.

8. RETAIN A POSITIVE ATTITUDE:

Whenever possible, associate with positive people. This is the worst possible time to allow those who tend to be negative, to influence your thinking. Keep looking for jobs, keep applying and sending your resume to companies and staffing agencies.

9. REMEMBER THAT THERE IS A WORLD OF OPPORTUNITY OUT THERE.

Whether you are facing a layoff (layoff) or are looking to make extra money while still working, you need to adjust your unique talents to suit the changing circumstances. Be creative in your thinking. Most people have (hidden) talents that they never use. Make a list of the things that you enjoy and are good at doing. Look at your hobbies to see if you can turn something that was / is a past time into a money generating activity. Ask yourself or ask your friends what do they think you are good at? Also learn new skills, such as computer skills and get certifications in your field.

Can you teach - can you motivate people? Can you purchase items and later resale them? Do you have enough money to consider flipping houses?

The Real Estate Industry: The world population keeps increasing and as long as there are people there will be needs for shelter. Real Estate is something to really consider if you have the means to invest in it. All you must do is, to study that industry and learn from other experienced people. You will have to learn how to negotiate price and how to select houses with potentials. Be able to work with good and affordable contractors to repair the properties for you. You will have to learn how to select correct locations to invest in. The Real Estate industry is one that has created a tremendous number of millionaires.

CHAPTER 12

A SELECTION OF OPTIONS FOR MAKING EXTRA MONEY

I. CARING FOR COMPANION ANIMALS

Most people living in first world countries like North America keep domestic (and sometimes wild) animals as pets.

Dogs and cats are by far the most popular companion animals, but parrots and in certain instances, less well-known animals such as pot-bellied pigs and miniature horses, are also kept. Animals need attention daily and for this reason a niche market has grown up around the caring of pets while their owners are on vacation or on business trips or even in hospital. Certain states and cities are pet-friendly. Cities like: Orlando, Florida, Tampa, Dallas, St. Louis, Birmingham, etc. are pet-friendly. In fact, it is very hard to go wrong in many parts of the USA with the pet industry. The pet industry is thriving because it is said that 75% of people in their thirties have dogs.

WHAT CAN YOU EXPECT TO BE DOING IN GENERAL IF YOU TAKE
CARE OF A PET FOR SOMEONE?

- **FEEDING AND WATERING:** Virtually all pets, except for reptiles, require daily feeding and access to clean and fresh water.

- **CLEANING UP:** As companion animals normally do not run free in the neighbourhood but are confined to a garden or in many cases to the house itself. The drawback is, you will need to clean up faeces daily and in the case of cats, empty their litter tray.
- **EXERCISING:** In the case of dogs, many owners will request that you take the dog out for a walk on a regular basis.
- **GROOMING:** Depending on the length of time that the owner will be away for, you may be required to groom animals as well.
- **VISITS TO THE VET:** Companion animals that become ill during their owner's absence, will require veterinary attention.

DOGS:

Dogs are favorite companion animals and range in size from the tiny "toy breeds" such as the Yorkshire Terriers and Maltese to giant types such as the Great Dane and Wolf Hound.

Although all dog breeds require exercise, the miniature types will get their required amount by simply playing within the house. Large dogs though need a reasonable walk or run every day. Many dogs that do not receive the correct amount of exercise, will find other outlets for their spent-up energy and become destructive by digging or chewing on non-acceptable house hold items.

Dog breeds that have long coats require regular brushing, which depending on the size of the dog may be time consuming.

Showing pedigree dogs in "breed shows", which are in effect beauty contests, have become a very popular hobby in America. The American Kennel Club (AKC) has registers more than 1 million dogs most years. A standard of perfection exists for each dog breed that is recognized and registered by the American Kennel Union and dogs are shown "against" these standards at shows around the country. It is not uncommon for owners and breeders of show dogs to appoint people to show their dogs for them and this is another opportunity to earn additional income (and possibly travel to some extent as Championship shows are held throughout the country and serious show folk, attempt to have their dogs represented at as many events as possible.

If you become involved with showing dogs on behalf of their owners, you may be required to:

- Groom or take the dogs (long hair breeds) for grooming / trimming to a specialist parlour before the event.
- Become involved with a certain amount of pre-show training. This normally involves conditioning the dog to stand still in the stance required for the specific breed and to allow the judge to touch him/her and open his/her mouth to check bite (teeth placement).
- Accompany the dogs to and remain with them during the show (normally a day but may spread over two days).
- Show the dogs. Dogs will run (walk for many toy breeds) around the judge and both towards and away from the judge, so that their gait (movement) can be observed.
- Return the dogs to their home.

CATS AND OTHER PETS:

Although cats are far more independent than what dogs are and do not require exercise, you will need to supply food and water and may be required to lock them into the house for either during the day or the night.

Parrots are highly intelligent birds that require regular attention to prevent them from becoming destructive. Parrots that become board may also begin to over groom their feathers and then to pluck themselves. This very bad habit is difficult to break once the bird has begun and owners will not be impressed with you if such behaviour begins on your "watch", so follow instructions carefully.

Reptiles have become very popular pets in North America, with different species of snakes normally being kept. Constrictors, which are the non-venomous types that squeeze their prey to death, are common, but venomous species are also occasionally found in private collections, so be sure to check on the type of snake if you are required to clean its cage or change water bowls or feed it.

2. House sitting

Looking after people's homes while they are away on business or vacation is an (often) fun and relatively easy to generate money.

House sitting may involve living in the other person's home for a period, or it may simply mean that you will be required to check on the house once or twice daily, to turn lights on or off, collect mail and /or to water indoor plants (or gardens).

Making extra money through your hobby.

Whatever your passion, be it making jewelry, creative painting, pottery or gardening, there are opportunities to generate additional income through creating items for sale at craft markets or similar venues.

If you become a self-employed artist, you will no longer have the worry of one day receiving a pink slip and loosing your job due to layoff. Apart from making your own living, you can be creative daily, which is extremely rewarding.

People who have a passion for something, soon become experts on most aspects of their chosen hobby and this the perfect background for a budding entrepreneur.

That having been said though, it is important to identify where your strongest skills lie.

So how would you begin? The first step involves researching the market. Although nobody enjoys writing up business plans, a modest plan is essential if you are going to succeed. It is going to take some serious work to turn your passion into profit and you will need to begin thinking like a businessman.

- **Conduct a market and competitive analysis:** You will need to know how much competition you are going to have. Depending on the number of your potential clients, there may already be an over supply of the "product" that you will be offering.
- **Design a marketing plan:** Check on the availability and affordability of the raw materials that you are going to use. Look into stockpiling the initial batches so that you have sufficient items

to sell, should the product sell well. Insure that you have sufficient time to continue after the first batch/s to keep momentum going. Be aware of transport costs if you need to need to take (large and heavy) items to craft markets or stores. Understand that you need to market and promote your products in some or other fashion (website / posters / adverts in local newspapers). Register with your states taxation office. Inquire whether you require a Business licence, Seller's Permit or Resale License. Create a PayPal account through which you can receive payments from long distance buyers.

- **SOURCE A MENTOR:** Finding a person who will be willing to guide and advise you, will be extremely helpful.

- **GUARD AGAINST BURNOUT:** In many respects you will now be approaching your hobby as a business and you need to guard against being involved 24/7. You may need to find or begin an entirely different hobby, to find a pleasurable outlet for fatigue and frustrations that may set in during the initial start up of your new business adventure.

- **BECOME PROFESSIONAL:** If you are serious about generating income from home, it is best to set up an office in your house. This need be nothing more than a table and chair in the corner of a room (preferably in your study or a spare bed room where you will not be disturbed too frequently). Apply for a separate "business phone". Remember that professional business starts with the image that you and your "business" projects. It is best therefore; that the children or others in the house do not answer the business calls. Depending on the type of home business that you plan to set up, a website, dedicated e-mail and fax line, will all be advantageous.

ART, CRAFT AND HOBBY OPTIONS.

Many folks have multiple interests, so it is important to identify where your strongest skills lie.

If you are to make money on a sustainable basis, it is important to approach your craft as a professional. Whatever you create therefore needs to be durable and of the highest quality possible. The paint you use should therefore no fade easily and wooden items should not easily fall apart.

Attempt to create "signature" items products that are totally unique to you and one which the buyer will eventually be able to identify as having been created by you. The more unique an item is, the more chance that it will stand out among similar products in the store or at a craft market.

PAINTING: Although you may enjoy painting in a specific style, attempt to diversify a little, as not everyone may have the same tastes as what you do.

Getting your name "out there", is a priority and one way of doing so, is to do a certain amount of your work in a busy park or shopping centre. Most people buy with their "eyes" and many people who watch an artist at work, particularly if the painter is creating portraits, show interest in commissioning one for them. Creating portraits of not only people, but of their pets as well, will help you diversify to attract more business.

Visit your local gallery to request that they exhibit your work and leave flyers with your contact details nearby. Include relevant and or interesting aspects of your background and discuss the different paint mediums that you use.

Create a website if possible to advertise the paintings that you have for sale and include articles about your style of painting and discuss paintings that you have already sold.

Check out the various online auction sites, particularly those that cater to an international audience.

Network as much as possible. Join relevant art groups and become as active as possible (consider starting your own group if necessary). Being part of a group makes you far more visible and enhances your chances of learning additional and new techniques that will improve your painting. Use the group to spread the word about the items that you have for sale.

ART POTTERY: Pottery is quite possibly the most popular of all crafts, mainly because the various items can be both functional and decorative. Although this section mainly discusses the selling of pottery, everything that you read here could as easily be used to sell paintings or any other craft item.

Create outlets wherever possible. Become acquainted with as many dealers and store owners as possible. Subscribe to any newsletters that are relevant and become a member of any group or club that deals with pottery in your area. Begin to check web sites on a regular basis, both from the point of looking to buy new stock and naturally from the point of checking the market for potential buyers.

Become known in the community as "the" person to approach for pottery. Learn as much as possible about all aspects related to pottery and pass your knowledge on freely. Arrange to give free lectures relating to pottery. The fact that these are offered without a charge, is not a problem, because you will be drawing many potential clients to yourself. You will have a captive audience and can ensure that each one leaves with you your contact details and any other relevant information regarding potter sales (from yourself).

Try to ensure repeat sales from the same people by always maintaining good relations with each of your clients. Contact them on a regular basis and check if there are any new pieces that they may require.

If you are selling your pottery at a craft market, arrange the various pieces in a pleasing fashion. Attempt to showcase the individual items so that each is shown off in the best possible way.

Since many pottery items will be used as functional pieces of equipment in the kitchen, always ensure that the one that you make for sale can withstand the wear and tear that being placed in a dishwasher places on them.

The pottery that you sell could be purchased from elsewhere initially, but if you are creative or are already involved with pottery and ceramics as a hobby, you can make your own items for sale. Although making pottery requires certain skills, these can be learnt and if you already have the basic equipment; the potter's wheel and kiln, you will be well on you way to begin a home business or be able to supplement your existing salary. If you require additional training in pottery (or any other art form for that matter), it is always possible to "trade out" skills. You could teach a new skill to the person who gives you lesson in advanced pottery techniques for example and in this way, this training will not cost you any money.

- **ANTIQUE ART POTTERY:** It is a strange truth that in most instances, "the rich get richer and the poor get poorer". Therefore, even in times of recession, many of the wealthy continue to buy luxury items and art pottery is one of the items that such buyers often look for. Collectors of art pottery are also known to pay exorbitant prices for certain pieces and select pieces may fetch more than $100.000. If you are interested in dealing in antique art pottery, you will need to become very familiar with the more well-known artists and companies that produced the various pieces. You will have to learn how to evaluate condition and develop a feel for the market for individual pieces (is it increasing or decreasing?). Although it may sound daunting at first, everything that has been mentioned is doable and if you eventually develop an eye for antique art pottery pieces, you could make a significant amount of money reselling pieces that you have purchased.

CHAPTER 13

Ongoing Options

Making money as a handy man.

During any economic recession, people immediately look for ways to save money. Folks, who previously would throw out old or damaged pieces of equipment or appliances, will in difficult financial times, choose to have these items repaired, if possible.

If you are in any way handyman orientated, you can capitalize on people's needs to repair appliances and set yourself up to offer this service.

Apart from doing the required work personally, you can also teach people how to repair their own items. Design a "do-it-yourself" website through which you instruct people how to repair the more common household or garden appliances.

Most people would be more comfortable doing than writing an instruction manual for others and there is nothing wrong with that. If you are serious about earning money as a handy man, you will need:

- The necessary skills (depending on the tasks that you intend to tackle – wood work, electrical, mortar and brick laying and so forth).
- Great customer service skills - Most people make the mistake of thinking that each individual industry revolves mainly around the technical aspects of what is manufactured, made or produced.

Businesses should revolve mainly around people and in particularly, around the client or customer. One of America's great Zoological Garden Directors, William Conway once said that he and his staff were not so much in the animal business as what they were in the people business. Conway meant that even though zoos were all about animals, without the paying public, they could not easily exist and so zoos had to become and remain very people oriented. The same is true of handy men (or, as mentioned, any other job).

- The desire and ability to network – It is important to get to know other people in a similar line of work. By communicating with them, you will get to hear valuable information regarding your clients (who takes forever to pay or is particularly difficult and so on). Knowing other handy men will help if you require assistance with a job that is too large for you to handle yourself. Get to know suppliers and contractors as well. These people are in the know and may be able to point you in the direction of your next job.

- Insurance – An insurance policy will cover you in the event of injury. Many of your clients may also prefer to only hire handy men that are covered by insurance.

- A licence – Be sure to check on the legal aspects of your new line of work. Your local building codes authority will direct you to the necessary licences, should they be required.

- Tools – Most of your clients will be looking to hire a handy man that has his own tools. You will come across as being more professional and may even be able to request more for the job or project if you can supply the tools that will be required. Your collection of tools can be build up over a period, but you should at least begin with a selection of all purpose tools such as a good quality drill (with an assortment of bits) and various saws.

The handy man is probably the original "jack of all trades" and the more knowledge you have or can build up, the more work you are likely to receive. Remember that the quality of your work will lead to repeat business from original clients, who will also "sing your praise" and by word of mouth, spread the news of your capabilities.

Always be honest with your clients. If you are not comfortable doing a specific job, or not skilled enough to handle it, speak up. Your customers will thank you for being honest and call on you at a later stage to complete work that you are familiar or expert at.

Attempt to retain a similar price for jobs that are alike and be careful not to bid too low. Many people are under the misconception that if they bid low, they will get the job. You may indeed be awarded the project, but if you do not make a profit on the work that you have preformed, you will have achieved nothing.

Remember to include Labor costs (if you intend to use additional staff for the job) and transport costs. These should be not only for your trips to the work site, but the (often numerous) small trips that you may be required to do while on the job (collecting pieces of equipment and or additional material as necessary).

BEGINNING A LANDSCAPING BUSINESS FROM HOME.

As previously mentioned, the wealthy among us strive to maintain their lifestyle, even during difficult financial times. Financially well-off folks tend to have and enjoy large and lavish gardens, which normally include water features, ponds and huge expanses of well maintained lawns and flower beds (of interest, the need for landscaping services is growing quicker than the national average for any other occupation). Someone needs to be responsible for the upkeep of such gardens and if you have a flare for plants and nature, that person could be you.

Landscaping encompasses a combination of living elements such as trees, grass and flowers with all the external elements of a well-planned garden, such as paths, decks, ponds, patios and lighting. Wherever you look in "A – income" areas, you will see examples of landscaping, ranging from residential properties, through public parks and golf courses to the gardens surrounding the civic centre or similar buildings.

If you are completely new to landscaping, you will need to do a good amount of serious reading, but fortunately, like many things in life, a person can learn the technical aspects of laying out an aesthetically pleasing garden and learn how to maintain the same. Those who are starting out in the landscaping business should look for residential projects to begin with before moving on to commercial projects.

As in the case all other work from home businesses, there are numerous methods to advertise yourself, but in the case of residential projects, word of mouth from satisfied clients, normally works best. You can also canvass for work door to door and distribute flyers. Obtaining commercial work normally requires one to place advertisements in either the local newspapers or business magazines.

Always arrive promptly if you are required to give a quote or are bidding (against others) on a project. Even though you will be working (or supervising) outdoors, always look and dress in a presentable manner. Carry a clipboard with and makes notes as the client speaks. It will not do to forget an important request or to misunderstand an instruction.

Landscape projects may require you to design and lay out a pleasing garden for your client, or they may involve the routine maintenance of existing gardens. As mentioned, most gardens include one or more water feature and many of these will have either goldfish or koi.

A minimum requirement for your business will be a light delivery vehicle or small truck, ideally with a trailer. Garden maintenance equipment such as lawn movers, rakes, spades and the like, also make up part of your (very) basic requirements, but hauling and clean up tools and equipment, will also be necessary.

What the work entails:

Planting and maintaining trees – These are the "flag ship" species in the garden. Most are very tall and impressive and will form focal points around which the smaller shrubs and flower beds are grouped. You will need to know about tree selection (watch out for aggressive root systems near buildings), correct planting methods, pruning, diseases of trees and how to both water and fertilize optimally.

Planting and maintaining grass – The grass will unite a garden; pull all the elements together so to speak. There are many different species of grass and their uses vary as ell; some types are best planted in shady areas, while other species are more resistant to drought and so on. You will be required to have knowledge about watering, the addition of fertilizers, diseases of grass (and pests that are associated with grass) and how best to mow and trim.

Planting and maintaining flower beds – You will require knowledge of soil types and plant nutrition. It will be necessary to know about seasonal planting and plant diseases, as well as about watering and weeds.

More and more people are becoming ecological friendly and many of your clients will insist on eco-landscaping, which involves water – efficient planting, integrated pest control and a generally self-sustaining development.

A landscape business can offer work all year long, as each season has its own requirements and special challenges. There will be a time for planting and a time for pruning, a time to water and watch growth and another when dead leaves will need to be raked and removed. There will be a time to clear away snow and source and supply Christmas trees.

MAKING MONEY AS A BABYSITTER

Most families have children and at some or other point, will require someone to take care of them for varying periods and this creates a demand for good babysitters.

Baby and child sitting is however a responsible job that will require commitment, considerable patience and a sound understanding of how young people think and behave.

- If you are starting out as a potential babysitter, it makes sense to accompany a friend on one of their "sitting shifts", to experience exactly what to expect when you are called upon to take care of a young person.
- Try to meet with the parents (or at least mother) of the child or children that you will be taking care of, prior to the actual sitting. This will give you the opportunity to be briefed by the mom and to get an "understanding" of how easy or difficult the children are going to be to get along with. Always take notes of the points raised by the mother. These are invariably extremely important facts and instructions that you can not afford to get wrong. Pay attention to any information related to medications that the children require to be given by you and be aware of any allergies that they may have. Ask if there are any foods that the children should not be given

and if you can let them play outdoors or take them for a walk or to the park. Check if their friends can come and play. Always stick to bed times as prescribed by the parents.

- As you will be taking care of their precious children, most families will be reluctant to source a babysitter through advertisements. This is one of the jobs through which you can benefit from word of mouth praise.

- Always negotiate fees upfront so that you there are not misunderstandings after you have completed the babysitting assignment.

- It is a good idea to bring a book to read, although it most homes, you will be allowed to watch the television or a DVD (normally with the children until it is time for them to go to bed). Be very wary of falling asleep. Parents will not be best pleased to arrive home and find their babysitter sleeping.

If you find that you enjoy babysitting, you may consider opening a modest day centre at your home, where parents can leave pre-school children or their young ones while they are out shopping or visiting.

Looking after young people can be very rewarding, both emotionally and financially.

Making money as a fish keeping consultant

Although dogs and cats are by far the most popular companion animals, millions of North Americans keep fish because an aquarium can fit into even a small apartment, whereas dogs and cats may not be allowed in many buildings or apartment blocks.

Although most people will keep a tank of tropical freshwater fish, more and more folks are taking the plunge and venturing into marine fish keeping. Marine or coral fish demand a more stable water quality than what freshwater fishes do and depending on the species, may require rather specialised feeding.

Because so many people are keeping fish tanks and most of these people will be on vacation or away from home on business at some point, you could make a tidy sum by making your services available as a fish tank consultant. In many cases, the people who have fish tanks, particularly large tanks, do not have the time or the interest (or knowledge) to maintain these aquariums, and this then becomes another aspect of the hobby that you can earn money from.

What maintenance work will be required on an aquarium?

- Your first task will be to remove the algae that grow continually on the glass of an aquarium due to nutrients (left over food and fish waste) in the water and light (tank's overhead lights and light in the room). This alga looks unsightly and if left for long enough, will hinder a person's view of the fish.
- Depending on how long it has been since the tank had a partial water change, you might have to drain an amount of aquarium water into a bucket or container and replace it with fresh water, to which you have added the necessary chemicals to remove chlorine that is invariably in the tap water.
- You will need to feed the fish and observe that they are all eating. During this time, check that they are swimming normally and behaving in the manner best suited to their type.
- Depending on the instruction that are left, you may also be required to clean one or more of the filters and replace whatever filter material is being used.

Goldfish and the large, normally very expensive koi (domesticated Japanese carp) are equally popular with American's today. These are traditionally kept outdoors in pond, which also require regular maintenance, so remember to advertise your services not only for indoor aquariums, but for outdoor ponds as well.

During a recession you need to concentrate on two extremely important factors; firstly, to source ways in which you can generate additional income and secondly (and as importantly) you need to find ways that you can save money. It is the people who can combine both approaches successfully, who will best survive the hardships of a recession. So before continuing with additional options to generate funds, let's take a quick look at saving as much as possible. Implement these ideas as soon as possible, so that you can begin saving immediately.

An old African saying asks how a pigmy (diminutive race of black Africans) can eat an elephant and the answer is "bit by bit". The saying is true of surviving a recession as well. As with most things in life, you don't always have to achieve great things each day, but if you work steadily at achieving a small victory on a regular basis, you will soon have attained a great victory after all. So, when it comes to saving during a recession, look for every way possible to save a little on an ongoing basis.

PAYING FOR PARKING: There are frequently more legal parking paces available on the street than what one might believe. We tend to prefer parking in the dedicated parking areas of malls and large stores to escape poor weather (rain, snow heat) and because it is convenient (close enough that we don't have to walk or carry our shopping bags too far), but such parking costs money, which if you make a note of, amounts to a fair amount each month. Look for legal parking bays in the street and save.

BANKING FEES: You will be surprised how quickly banking fees add up. Be aware of what you are charged for by your bank and take steps to cut costs on bank fees wherever possible.

- ATM fees - It costs more to withdraw cash if you are not making use of an auto teller that is dedicated to your specific bank. Always draw down cash from your own bank's ATM, unless you are banking with a financial institution that offers free ATM usage.
- Checks and postage – Where possible, save money by making payments electronically.
- Overdrafts – Link the various cards that you have so that you will be able to address any "insufficient fund" issues by electronically transferring money as required. In this way, you will be able to avoid paying any "penalty" fees.
- Most TD Bank branches count coins for free, which will save you the cost of having small change counted at the supermarket.

WARRANTIES: Very few items today come without a warranty option and although such options make sense, they may simply become a luxury during very difficult financial times. You could certainly consider waving the warranty on the cheaper appliances that will need to be replaced shortly in any event. Wherever possible, try not to take out insurance on items that really do not require it.

GENERAL INVESTING ADVICE: Most people do not believe that they have the necessary knowledge to arrange their own financial planning and tend to look toward the services of a professional financial planner. This may be all well and good, but during a recession or when you have been laid off work, these costs may fall into the luxury category.

Without too much effort at all, most people will be able to use the many software programs that are available to assist them with decisions regarding investments. In other words, you can build your own financial portfolio and save on the costs of having an outsider do so on your behalf.

CREDIT REPORTS: Unfortunately, very little in life is free. Be wary of internet sites that advertise "free" credit reports for example. Many of these sites may supply you with a complementary report, only to encourage you to take part in a (normally) costly monitoring program. You can request a free report from a credit bureau and it is a god idea to do so on a quarterly basis, so that you can monitor your credit status regularly.

ONLINE SHOPPING: Take a look at www.FreeShipping.org, where you can invariably find seriously discounted or free delivery from a huge number of retailers. Some of these may be short term promotions, but many offers are permanent.

RENTAL VEHICLE INSURANCE: In a perfect world, taking out insurance on your rental vehicle, simply makes good sense. During difficult financial times, this could b considered a luxury though. The rental company is out to make a large a profit as possible and most will not tell you that if the rental is for your private use, the collision coverage in your own auto – insurance policy, will cover you. Remember also that your credit card benefits will assist with auto coverage.

STUDENT AID: Make use of the U.S. Department of Education's official site, as opposed to any commercial site, when applying for your student aid. The government site is free and completely informative.

CHAPTER 14

STARTING AN INTERNET BUSINESS

It is a sad reality that few people can rely on companies to provide work and job security for them into the (even immediate) future. Even people who are prepared to accept lower wages, work flexible hours and function in other areas of the company, are no longer guaranteed their jobs.

Today though, with personal computers being so popular, most people could begin an internet marketing business if they so choose.

USING THE INTERNET TO BEAT TOUGH TIMES.

Internet marketing, if approached correctly, can be a very profitable home business to "break into". The great secret to success with internet marketing is to create multiple streams of income and it is this approach that you will learn about in chapter four and several the following chapters.

DON'T BE TOO CONCERNED ABOUT A FINANCIAL OUTLAY.

No one is keen to spend extra money during a recession or after you have been laid off work, so the thought of having to pay someone to design and build a website for you, most probably is not very appealing.

Fortunately, most people, with a little assistance, can do a perfect job of building their own website and this is exactly what I am going to show you in this chapter.

AFFILIATE MARKETING: creating and selling your own products can be a difficult and even risky venture. One way of getting around this problem, is to become active in affiliate marketing. By offering other companies the opportunity to expose and promote their products on your website; you can earn commission, which can become lucrative.

If approached correctly, you can effectively generate sufficient money to continue making a good living, if you have already been retrenched or laid off. Some of the many advantages of affiliate marketing are that you can have your own business without requiring an inventory or having to incur any substantial overheads. The majority of "online" companies offer "affiliate programs", through which you will be able to promote that companies products and earn money in doing so. Promoting the services or products of other companies, can become highly profitable.

AFFILIATE PROGRAMS: You would need to "join" an affiliate program on a website and then link this program to your own website (you will receive a unique affiliate link and identification number). You then briefly review a few their products and drive visitors that are on your own site to the other company or "merchants" official sales page, by using your affiliate link – "click to learn more".

SEARCH ENGINE OPTIMIZATION (SEO): Several your visitors will invariably end up purchasing one or more items from the other company and as they have clicked through your affiliate link, you will receive a commission on their purchase (normally in the region of 50%).

The secret to making serious money through affiliate marketing, is to get as many people visiting your website as possible and this you achieve through using the appropriate "keywords or phrases" relevant to the products that you want your visitors to purchase from the merchant's sales page. In internet "jargon" you would speak of gaining a high ranking for these keywords and the process involved to assure this ranking, is termed Search Engine Optimization (SEO).

Your first vital step is to optimize your website for search engines to easily locate you and to then easily be able to explore the information that you present. In the simplest of terms, you require the correct keywords to be found by the search engines of the world. Look at your competitor's websites at this point to get a better understanding of why they are doing well (that is if they are naturally).

Don't proceed any further until you have optimized all the necessary keywords. The success or failure of you site rides upon this crucial step.

DOMAIN NAME:

Once you have chosen the correct keywords, you will be ready to purchase a domain name. This is your hostname, sometimes also referred to as your URL and identifies you among a world wide web of people. Always attempt to have this name include your most important keywords, as such, will help with search engine optimization. Although you will be building your own website, there are still a few costs that you will need to pay and obtaining your website address is one of these. Fortunately, domain names will not cost you an arm and a leg and tend to cost below $20.00 annually. Key the domain name as short and simple as possible.

Once you are satisfied that all your keywords have been chosen correctly, you need to begin "building" your website. Remember that you will be competing on a global platform, so your site needs to be ultra appealing to visitors (and to search engines). Building on your site is never really finished, in that you will want to continually update the information to keep it current and may want to add or delete "sections" as you go or as the site matures and possibly changes focus. It is important to ensure that any new information that you add, keeps to your original theme.

Attempt to add at least one article per week and always use appropriate keywords. You will also find free articles (in many cases republishing is allowed) available on an article directory website and by carefully working through these, you are bound to find suitable material for your own use.

INDEXING YOUR WEBSITE: You are now ready to have your website indexed, which you can achieve by requesting another website to link to yours. Attempt to source a top-ranking website as your first link, to speed up the indexing process. If the site that links to you has a high enough rating, your website should be indexed within two days. This process may take longer however, and you should be prepared to wait a week or two if necessary.

HOSTING YOUR WEBSITE: Once you have created the basic website, you will be ready to have it hosted by one of the many companies that offer this service.

You should track your website details (links to affiliate programs / query statistics / where your traffic is coming from / how long they are browsing for / which of your keywords were used to find you and the like).

Sign up for a free Google Analytics Account to access this information.

All the steps that have been mentioned are extremely important to ensure that your site is of a sufficiently high standard to attract the necessary traffic, for it is this traffic that will generate your money.

E-MAIL MARKETING: This internet marketing tool is a means whereby you can communicate with potential clients through e-mail correspondence (normally making use of newsletters or auto responders).

- SET UP AN AUTOMATIC E-MAIL RESPONDER - You would need to set up automatic e-mail responder (which is just a special e-mail address) which will automatically forward (pre-stored) messages of your choice to people who initially click on that address. You would invite a potential subscriber to sign up for your product by entering their e-mail address (and possibly more information, such as their name and residential address) in an op-in box on your website.

   The automatic e-mail responder then continues to send out pre-stored messages of your design to these "clients" reminding them about your product and inviting them to purchase. Your newsletter (promoting the product/s of your choice) can be included in these automated responses.

   The great secret behind e-mail marketing is to build relationships with your potential clients. You need to create an element of trust before most people will begin to buy your products, so do not attempt a "cold sale" in the first few mails. Through the accompanying newsletter, offer advice of value through which you begin to build a "relationship" with this (hopefully) long term client.

- **DON'T EVER SPAM** - People today are becoming increasingly aware of and resentful about receiving "spam mail". Do not ruin your chances of ongoing sales by being the cause of your clients receiving spam mail. Indicate in your first message to them that you will not use their e-mail address for any other purpose than to communicate with them personally. Do not then give (or sell) their address to anyone else that may then pass it on further or may begin spamming them.

- **BE AWARE OF YOUR WORDING** - The e-mail service will be automatically triggered to either block your message or to send it to the client's spam box, if it detects certain words. These words include: free / discount / great offers / call now / order now / while supplies last / time limited and similar concepts.

- **SOURCE THE CORRECT AUTO RESPONDER SOFTWARE** – By using this software, you will be able to gauge how many people are looking at what you have written and where these folks are located. Look for software that is both user-friendly and realistically priced and source software that does not require that you pay monthly service fees. Always purchase the option that offers a once off payment.

If you are diligent in following the required steps, there is no reason to believe that you will not be successful at marketing through the internet.

Internet marketing involves far more than the points that have already been covered though and in the next and following chapters, I will introduce you to many more details of this (very) profitable venture.

Dream Boards: By way of concluding this chapter, I would like to encourage you to create a "Dream Board".

I was going to write that even adults should dream but want to change this to "it is particularly adults that should dream". You need to have a vision of where you want to be financially and one practical step to keep this "dream" alive in your mind, is to create a dream board.

Think about all the various things that are important to you during this financially difficult time; you may desperately want to keep up payments so as not to lose your home or you may still want to purchase your spouse a birthday gift, despite having been laid off work.

Write these needs / dreams - down on a board that you place in your bedroom or kitchen and add appropriate pictures as well. Look at what you are striving to achieve daily and tell yourself that despite the current financial situation, you will succeed. Ensuring a positive frame of mind is crucial during times of crisis. Use your board to remind you of what you are working towards and never give up hope.

CHAPTER 15

NON-WEBSITE VENTURES

Despite its popularity and (almost) international appeal, the internet remains daunting to may people. Affiliate marketing as discussed in chapter four, may not suite everyone because of the technical aspects that a person needs (or believes that they need) to master.

Fortunately, a person can begin with non-web related marketing, which immediately cuts out the need to have your own website and all that such marketing entails.

Non-web related marketing methods, if approached correctly, can be very profitable (and can offer long-term financial benefits), so look at this chapter and see if anything interests you.

Money from forums: Forums are immensely popular gathering places for people from all over the world. People enjoy writing about themselves, their hobbies and occupations. They ask questions of others and answer questions from others and this situation offers you a wonderful opportunity to become involved. You too can give advice and, in the process, promote a service that you are offering or discuss a product.

Sign up with the affiliate program from a site whose products you would like to promote. You will receive your affiliate website address which you will use to promote the products. A person should ideally have personally used (or at least tried out) the products that you will promote, to give an honest appraisal of their effectiveness.

Source your online forums now and join up. Be cautious though not to simply rush in a begin promoting your product. The best approach will be to participate in the discussion initially. Become known a little, which will help with your credibility and try to make a few online friends on the site.

Create a signature to end off each post that you write and, in the signature, create a link to your affiliate program. Anyone and everyone on the forum who looks at your contribution, can click on the link and thereafter (hopefully) purchase one or more of the products that you are promoting. Search engines will also pick up you link, which means that people who are busy with an internet search, will be directed to your link.

As in any life scenario, be aware of forum etiquette. Check to see if the forum that you are planning to join, allows affiliate links and if this is not the case, you do not need to waste valuable time by joining and posting in order to become known. Observing online etiquette is as important if you do join a forum. Always make sure that you follow any and all rules as stipulated by the moderators of the site.

Social Networking - Refers to people online working as a team toward business or social objectives. These people, regardless of their geographical location, can share ideas and interests by being connected to the internet.

Although many people use such networks (Face book for example) to socialise, it is also possible to use them for business purposes (money generating). These sites become somewhat addictive, so you can be assured of online users almost constantly.

Source groups that have an interest in the products that you are "dealing" in and begin to establish yourself as an authority in that particular "field".

Writing: If you are in any way creative and enjoy writing, you can supplement an existing salary or earn money after a layoff or during difficult financial times, by writing articles and selling these through various internet sites.

- **Making money as a Freelancer** - Join one of the many freelancers' websites and create a profile for you. Some sights offer free membership but deduct a percentage of your earnings from each job (anywhere from 3% to 10%) that you will be rewarded.

Once you are signed up, you will receive regular announcements of jobs that "buyers" around the globe require to be done. You will need to bid against an international audience of freelance writes, which can be daunting initially, but becomes less so after you have been awarded your first few jobs.

- **Create an account** - You will need to create an account (such as PayPal) into which your earnings can be paid and thereafter you should monitor the available jobs on as regular a basis as possible, bit for those that you believe you can do justice to and then simply get down to producing great work once you have been awarded a project.

WRITING AN E-BOOK:

Our technology is changing daily and there is a world of people all wanting to know about something or the other.

The internet has become a popular place for millions of people to source answers to questions that range for cooking recipes to medical advice, which makes today the perfect time for you to write one or more E-Books. If you have a passion for a hobby or craft, you could create a great recourse, which can be downloaded as an E-product or be published online as an E-Book.

E-Books: Writing an E-Book can be quite lucrative as you will not have and overhead costs. There are no printing fees (which are normally considerable in the traditional hard copy publishing business) or shipping and handling fees.

Although it is true that a great number of people might be interested in the subject that you want to write about, it is equally true that many books or articles on the subject, might already exist. It is for this reason that you will need to research the market to see what competition you have and to best gauge what unique angle your E-Book will need to take to be interesting enough for people to want to buy it.

- Who will your target market be? – When you write, you need to picture the people who will want to buy and read the work that you are creating. You need to understand what these "clients" will want to know about the subject.

- Know your subject very well – Those who ultimately buy or download the book that you are writing, will be genuinely looking to find advice and assistance within the pages and for this reason, you need to offer the best possible advice that is available. Do not therefore attempt to write an E-Book on any subject that you are not very well-versed in.

- Sales routes – Writing an E-Book will be a somewhat a time-consuming exercise and you should know how you are going to market the finished product. If you already have a website, this could be the perfect place to advertise and sell the book from. In addition to your own website, there are other internet outlets through which you can market and sell your book. One such venue is the E-BookMall. Each book that you sell through this outlet, will earn you money, but a percentage of the sale is retained by E-BookMall for allowing you to trade through their site. Clickbank and Plimus are two other popular outlets through which you can sell.

With all things being equal, if the information that you have included in your E-Book is sound and if you are able to market it through the venues that I have mentioned, there is no reason why you should not receive a fair amount of money for your efforts. Although you may be facing a recession in your own country because the internet is available to a global audience, people in other countries, who may not necessarily be experiencing difficult financial times, will still be buying your work.

CHAPTER 16

Regardless of what you ultimately decide to do to generate extra income during a recession or any other difficult financial time for that matter, it is always a good idea to stop every now and again and check that **you are still thinking smart and working to a plan.**

Design your business around your passions and interests

People who believe in what they do, inspire confidence in others and as these others will be your present and future clients, it makes sense to always approach whatever task you are attempting, to the very best of your ability.

Remember to always get the basics right: Here is a story to impress upon you how important it is to master the basic principles of every job you choose to do.

"A stationmaster (who is an official in charge of a railroad station). receives a phone call one evening to say that a bridge just east of his station has collapsed and that a train is fast approaching the station from the west, on route towards the broken bridge.

The stationmaster, dressed in only his gown, runs bare feet over the sharp stones that line the short road from his home to his office and grabs a lantern. He then rushes toward the train tracks and standing on the line, begins to frantically signal the oncoming train. The train does not slow down though, and the station master eventually throws himself from the railway tracks just seconds before the train hurtles past. It continues at speed on its journey and as could be predicted, plunges off the broken bridge, killing everyone in the process.

The station master is naturally found not guilty, as he did everything in his power, including risking his life, to stop the train, but he never recovers from the incident.

*One day, an old friend asks why he continues to brood over the events of that terrible night and the station master answers that none of the people who questioned him after the accident, ever asked **if there was a globe in the lantern***"

The sad moral to this story, is that no matter how hard you try and no matter what hardships you endure (and no matter how brave you are), if you do not get the basics of your business right, your mission is doomed to failure.

Invest in your new business

Even though you are working during a recession, put as much money as you can possibly afford back into your business.

Your new business will need to keep you afloat during these difficult financial times and you can not afford to have it collapse around you.

Do not be discouraged by negative people.

The world is full of pessimistic people and their negativity is never as obvious as during (very) difficult financial times. Do not let such people talk you out of a plan to begin a business or allow them to trash your dreams of succeeding. In fact, it is during such times (recessions and layoffs) that you should do everything in your power to associate only with the most positive people that you know.

Invest in stocks:

To invest in the stock market, you will need to get the help of a financial adviser or you need to create an account with a brokerage firm. You will need to have a certain amount of money to start. It depends on the firm's requirement. The minimum could be a $1000 or $2000.

You could invest in Mutual funds or bonds and for your mutual funds you can set it up at your local bank. Nowadays, you can find investment accounts starting at 100 to 500 dollars.

Diversification is great because it helps you reduce risks because you would be purchasing from a pool of stocks. One thing you need to remember is that extreme diversity in your portfolio is not always the best move. You can do your research and we what is the next telecom company, what company has been doing well for the past few years. Find out about the blue-chip companies, the great technology, communication and healthcare companies and invest in these companies.

CHAPTER 17

Back to pets and how to earn big money from small fishes

Although earning money from various internet businesses, can be very lucrative, not everyone has access to a computer and not everyone is comfortable using one. Many folks who did not take classes in computers at school or collage, may feel intimidated by the technology involved and prefer not to make use of this opportunity to generate money during a recession or after having been laid off.

Making money by using your computer also requires that you be connected to the internet, which will cost you money.

If you prefer not to consider computers and their related technology as money making venture, here is a proven way of generating good money without any technology involved.

People and pets: People in first world countries enjoy keeping companion animals of all descriptions. It may be of interest to know that in England although they have a *Society for the Prevention of Cruelty to Children*, they have a *Royal Society for the Prevention of Cruelty to animals*. People in North America are equally taken by their furry and feathered friends and the pet industry in the States is a multi billion-dollar affair.

Despite the huge popularity of the many different dog breeds, folk who live in single rooms or apartment blocks, may either choose not to have a dog, or may not be permitted to keep one. Even medium sized dogs require exercise and unfortunately often develop the habit o barking when left alone, which is bothersome to neighbours and normally results in the animal's owner being reported.

Although parrots, which are popular as companion animals, are smaller than virtually all dog breeds, they have the habit of screeching in a high-pitched voice, particularly if left alone for long periods. Parrots in the wild instinctively communicate by screeching and for this reason, it is almost impossible to train these birds not to vocalise. In the confines of an apartment building thought, this (often) continuous "calling" can become very disturbing to neighbours and parrots are therefore also not always welcome.

A pet for all occasions: For the reasons above, fish have become extremely popular as pets. The fact that a small aquarium or fish bowl can be kept in the tiniest of apartments, has pushed fish keeping as a hobby, right to the foreground.

And this is where the potential for making extra money during difficult financial times, comes in.

The problems associated with wild caught fish: There is an ongoing demand for all the various fish types that are commonly kept in the hobby and several fish species are still wild caught and shipped (at additional expense) from their areas of origin to the booming pet trade in first world countries. Wild caught fish are invariably stressed by the process of capture and transport and arrive at the dealer's shop in a weakened state. Many of these fish die shortly after reaching their destination, which is all too often the hobbyist's aquarium.

Wild caught fishes are also prone to disease, which they then introduce to a hobbyist's aquarium of otherwise healthy fish, after they have been purchases. Many wild caught fishes are also adult when captured and have been accustomed to feed on certain food items in their natural habitat, which are not easily replaced once they are in the aquarium.

The secrets of breeding fish for money: The more breeding or spawning tanks that you have, the younger fish you will be able to produce, but you can begin with as few aquariums as your available cash allows for.

Choosing which species to breed – guppies, mollies, platys and a host of other tropical fresh water fish types are very popular aquarium inhabitants and certainly worth breeding with, but their young will not fetch high prices. Today, more and more highly exotic and endangered fish types are being kept by hobbyists and the babies of these species do carry a considerable price tag. After becoming familiar with the basics of breeding the more common and hardy types like the guppy, you may seriously want to consider purchasing one or two pairs of the more expensive fish species. Always attempt to obtain young specimens, because these will be far less expensive and if correctly cared for, will be longer lived than adults, who may even be past their reproductive age when you buy them.

- **Discus** are exquisitely beautiful, plate shaped fish from the Amazon River and its tributaries. Although the wild discus has a somewhat drab brown colour, tank bred specimens are produced in the most striking hues, with names such as Red Dragon, Piebald and Cobalt Blue. Once the young of discus hatch, the (often) hundreds of babies feed on the body slime of their parents, which means that you do not need to worry about feeding the fry for some weeks. Discus require very soft (acidic) water, which you can create by adding peat to the filter compartment or by adding commercially available chemicals to lower the pH of the water to 6.8 or 6.9. Your discus breeding tank will need to be at least twenty gallons. Your discus youngster will fetch a good price and local per dealers will be quick to snap them up because high quality discus fish are not easily come by.
- **Oscars**, although not as expensive as discus, are a very popular fish species that also hails from the Amazon basin. These fish develop very definite personalities and are sometimes referred to as "tank busters" because of their belligerent nature. They remain popular though and have been bred in several "domestic" colours. Like discus, Oscars will require a large tank in which to breed and are normally ready to spawn by eighteen months of age. Oscars will lay their eggs on horizontal surfaces, so you will need to lay the slate flat on the aquarium floor. The eggs will hatch in three days and unlike discus, the parents may be tempted to eat either their eggs or their young. If you are unlucky enough to have such a pair,

they can be removed after egg laying to a display or "holding" tank. The tiny Oscars will live off their yolk sack for four days before requiring food.

- **Piranhas**, due to their fierce reputation, have become highly sought-after aquarium fish. Although it is illegal to keep these flesh-eating predators in many North American states, they are ordered in large numbers in areas where hobbyists are permitted to purchase them. Like the ocean-going sharks, piranha feed on other living creatures and as they travel in large schools and possess razor sharp teeth, a family or pack of piranhas can strip an animal to the bone in minutes. These fish are fortunately not as ferocious under captive conditions, but their reputation fascinates hobbyists sufficiently for a great many to want to keep them. Piranhas will pair off in your display tank, which needs to be eighty to one hundred gallons in volume. Once the pair establishes a territory and turns dark in colour, they will be close to laying eggs. Provide pieces of slate on which the female can deposit her eggs and remove the slate to one of your smaller spawning / hatching tanks. This tank should be filled with water from the parent's display tank. The young will hatch within four days and with careful attention to water quality and with regular feeding of crushed pellets and tiny pieces of ox heart, there is no reason why you can not raise a good batch of babies that will be eagerly snapped up by dealers and hobbyists alike.

Spawning tanks – for most species do not necessarily need to be very large. In fact, in nature the male fish need to protect both the territory that he has chosen to live in and his female or females. Once the eggs have been laid, he (and sometimes the female as well) will need to protect these, so most territories are relatively small in the wild. Your breeding tank can range from five gallons to thirty gallons (species dependant).

Additional equipment – you do not require much equipment in a spawning tank. For the most part, gravel can be dispensed with (which makes the tank easier to clean) and a piece of slate or upturned plant pot, can replace any aquatic vegetation that you might see in display tanks. The slate and pot will be used by the fish as breeding sites and eggs will be laid against either. The water in your tanks will need to be of a high quality and this is achieved by adding on or more filters to the aquarium. Because the young fish can easily be drawn into powerful filters, small internal "bubble" filters work best. Tropical fish species will require warm water, and this is easily achieved by placing an aquarium heater in each breeding tank.

Diet for your adult fish – the quality of your young fish will depend in no small way on the quality of your breeding stock and it pays therefore to feed the parents a balanced and nutritious diet. Many excellent commercial fish foods are available today, but these should be supplemented with a little frozen and live food to condition your brood stock. Frozen prawns or shrimps are an excellent food supplement, as are earth worms (night crawlers) that are cut to size.

Show me the money: Folks across the States are keeping fish of one description or another and pet dealers will be more than happy to purchase the fish that you have bred, particularly if they are of a high quality.

CHAPTER 18

Growing and selling vegetables

Vegetables make up the diet of a great many people in North America. If you have a small area of ground available and a little time on your hands, you can easily grow quality vegetables and make them available for sale. Using your own home-grown vegetables for personal consumption, will also cut done of food bills, which is exactly what you are looking for during difficult financial times.

Follow these simple rules and you will soon have your first delicious batch of fresh vegetables for personal use or for sale.

Source you compost: By carefully selecting such kitchen items as eggshells, peelings, used tea bags and wilted flower arrangements, you can make compost that does not cost you a penny.

Designate an area for your vegetable garden: Depending on the amount of space that you have available, measure out one or more vegetable beds that are roughly the size of a normal door. Your beds ideally need to be in a section of the garden that received a good deal of sun each day.

Prepare your vegetable beds: Loosen the soil in your bed and dig down by approximately half a metre. Remove most of the soil and replace this with the "compost items". Wet the bed at this point and then return the darker (richer) top soil until your bed is just slightly higher than the surrounding ground. Run a rake across the bed to level out any uneven areas of soil. Add a thin layer of "mulch", in the form of dry leaves. The mulch will protect the top soil from temperature fluctuations and conserve water.

Plant your seedlings: Create rows across your vegetable bed, by parting the mulch with a small trowel, or with your hands. Use a stick to then make shallow furrows from one side (width) of the bed to the other. Once you have your furrows, create "planting holes" by pushing your finger or stick approximately 1 cm into the soil for the smaller seeds and 2 cm for larger seeds. Smaller vegetable types can also be planted 20 cm apart, but the larger varieties such as cabbage, will require a planting space of at least 30 cm. Do not cover the seeds that you plant, as they will require both light and warmth from the sun to begin the process of germination.

Caring for your seeds: Water your seedling on a regular basis, particularly for the first week to ten days. Thereafter, water the seeds at least two to three times per week. At this stage, the gentle spray from a watering can is more seedling friendly than a strong spray from your hose pipe. One the young vegetable plants have reached a height of 10 cm, you can add additional mulch to the bed.

Harvesting your vegetables: Harvest your vegetables one row at a time. You can replace the vegetables that have just been removed, by immediately sowing new seeds in their place. It is also good gardening practice to rotate your vegetable crop, so replace your cabbage and lettuce (leaf crop) with vegetables such as potatoes, which is a root crop. Once you have harvested both leaf and root crops, you can plant legumes such as peas.

Be an environmentally friendly gardener: Consumers today are becoming increasingly aware of pesticides and hormones and a host of other unhealthy and potentially dangerous products that are sprayed onto food crops or fed to milk or beef cattle. One of your great "selling" points can be that you are supplying vegetables that have been grown and treated for pests organically. Avoid all pesticides and use only organic sprays on your vegetables.

- **Soapy water** - is probably the easiest of all eco – friendly pesticides to obtain because all you require is left over dish water. Spray this liberally onto the vegetables at least once weekly to keep most of the commonly found insect pests at bay.

- **Tobacco spray** - Mix at least a cup of tobacco into a one-gallon bucket of water and allow this to stand for a day. This mixture will keep most pests off your vegetables but is best not used on tomatoes and eggplants.

- **Garlic and onion spray** - Crush both a garlic bulb and a medium union and mix these with a gallon of soapy water. This mixture will keep not only the common insect pests at bay, but slugs as well.

An indoor vegetable garden: Apartments and homes without access to any type of garden are still suitable to produce sprouts. Sprouts are extremely healthy for you, as they contain numerous minerals, enzymes and vitamins. They can be added to dishes such as soups, casseroles and stews, or simple eaten in their raw state, by adding them to a salad

Place your seeds in a glass jar filled with water (with a lid containing holes) and leave them to soak overnight. Drain the water from the jar by pouring it out through the holes in the jar's lid and leave the seeds for up to five days. During this time, although they should not be in water, you must ensure that the seeds do not dry out either.

By the end of five days, the resulting sprouts will be ready to eat or to package for sale to neighbours and friends.

CHAPTER 19

Domestic services

There are many jobs around the house that require doing on a regular basis and none of them appeal to the rich and famous. Wealthy folk prefer not to have to wash and iron their own cloths, or to vacuum the rooms in their house or to make dinners.

Should you have been laid off work of are simply trying to make a little additional money during a recession, domestic work may be just the thing to bring in that extra cash.

Washing and ironing: Your clients may include busy moms who are just not able to cope, college students, disabled folk and pensioners who are still living in their on homes. You will probably need to place several advertisements initially, but once you have your first clients, you will be able to rely on their "word of mouth" references to "hook" progressively more and more customers

You will need you own washing machine and preferably your own vehicle for picking up and delivering the laundry, but once you have a few clients, your profits will be good.

Most folk who have their laundry washed, will require that it be ironed as well, but it is best to have separate prices for each, just in case. Some people are quite particular about they want their cloths ironed, so it is best to check on this when collecting the laundry.

Purchase your own plastic laundry baskets for the cloths of clients who do not leave one for you and be very careful not to mix up the laundry from different customers. If you have misplaced an item of clothing for whatever reason, be honest and mention this when you drop the laundry off. Most people will understand and will also appreciate your honesty. Normally, these so called lost items will show up again and can then be returned to their owner.

Always invoice your clients and be sure to carry sufficient small change with you for customers who pay when you drop their laundry off.

Cleaning homes: Just as some folk do not want to do their own laundry, so many do not want to do other house hold chores, such as washing the windows, dusting and vacuuming.

Setting yourself up to clean houses can become quite lucrative as well, because there will always be clients lining up to make use of your services.

CHAPTER 20

"I really want your business"

Although the main reason that you will be involving yourself with one or more of the businesses mentioned in this book is to generate extra money, you will quite probably not be the only person offering a service in that specific field. Yes, there is bound to be competition and possibly, a lot of it.

Even though you will be hoping to make as large a profit as possible, you may have to invest in several promotional techniques, if you are to beat off the competition.

Offer your clients something for free

As strange as this may sound, offering something for free is a sure-fire approach to be remembered by your clients and to keep your competitive edge.

Outstanding service: When all is said and done, offering quality service is without doubt the best sales promotion technique available. People are quick to notice and appreciate excellent service and when they do not receive it, are equally quick to spread the word around. If clients are speaking about you, you need to ensure that it in the most positive way possible.

Reduced fees: Everyone (yes, you and most certainly me) is always looking for "a great deal". Although you may not be able to offer a reduced price each time to sell an item or perform a service for your clients, attempt to do so on a one in ten bases and let it be known that you will consider negotiating a fee in certain cases. Happy customers will be quick to sing your praise and this type of "word of mouth" advertising is a powerful means to spread the word about your services.

Buy one get one free: The word "free" is one of the most powerful words that you will ever hear. Regardless of what you may be doing to earn extra money, you will be able to find a way to work this "guaranteed to be successful" promotion into your sales pitch. If you are babysitting for example, you can offer a free service for each paid session during a week or month. If you are maintaining a fish pond or mowing a lawn, you can offer the same deal.

Samples: These are only applicable if you are selling something but work very well nevertheless.

DEVELOP YOUR PEOPLE SKILLS

Regardless of how you are going to make extra money, you will invariably be dealing with people and unless you can do so in a professional manner, you are bound to lose business.

Be completely honest: Your clients will expect you to be totally honest with them. Regardless of the job that you are bidding on, whether it is laying a cement path, painting the garage roof, or building a fish pond, answer all questions put to you by the client honestly. If there are parts of the job that that you are not really qualified to do, indicate as much or have a person in mind that you can sub – contract to complete that part of the overall task.

Insist on a contract: We all instinctively want to trust people. After being awarded a job, you may be so thankful that you do not want to push the issue of a signed contract, particularly if the clients come across as decent folk, who gave you a cup of coffee and shook your hand on the deal. Life unfortunately does not always work on a "hand shake". If you are doing extra work to generate money, it is probably because you need that money to pay essential bills, such as your house rent or mortgage. It makes little sense therefore to spend your time (and in some cases, you own money) and not receive payment, or the full payment for work done.

Be aware of these points during your negotiations

- Let your customers know upfront that you will require a signed contract. This affords them the opportunity to walk away from the deal before too much time is wasted, should they not want to enter a concrete deal.
- Explain in detail your cost structure so that the customer can understand how their money is going to be spent.
- Try to agree on the smaller issues as early in the discussions / negotiations as possible, as this puts you and your client on the same wavelength and will help you both to see "eye to eye" on the much bigger issues pertaining to the job or contract.
- The initial verbal discussions or even agreement is always only the beginning. It is an overview of what lies ahead. The "devil is in the detail" and unless you lay the detail out in a signed contract, much can and normally does go wrong.
- Your clients (in fact everyone) buys items or services mainly out of laziness or greed. Try to work out which emotion is relevant in each of your cases, so that you know what drives that specific customer during that deal.

Stick to the time line: Once you have committed yourself to a completion date, ensure that you stick to it. Even if the job that you have been awarded is very small, your clients will have expectations regarding when it will be completed, particularly if you have indicated a specific date in the contract. Unhappy customers are going to spread negative comments about your work, which can only do your business damage.

Look the part: Once you have landed the job and are painting a roof or digging out a garden dam, there is no reason why you can not work in an overall or cloths that are suited to type of (dirty) work that you are performing, but always dress neatly when seeing the client for the first time and during subsequent negotiations. Your customers will want to know that they are working with a professional and will want their friends and neighbours to think (know) the same.

Be courteous and polite: It does not cost you anything to be polite and your manner of speaking is as important as your dress code if you want to indicate that you are professional. The guys may speak crudely when they are in an all male group at the bar, but these same people will normally not approve of bad or dirty language around their wife or children when you are in their home. This is particularly true if you are working for them.

CHAPTER 21

Additional tips on saving

Here are a few additional ides that will help you put a little extra money into your saving account every month.

Check your change: Small change is not worth very much today (as it is), but if you deposit all your change into a container at the end of every day, you will invariable have a good few dollars at the end of each month. Try to bank this amount (into a savings account) or failing that, use it for a very specific purpose, such as gas money for the first week (or two hopefully) of the new month.

Holiday in a friend's home: The home need not necessarily have to belong to a friend. What I am speaking about here, is house swapping. In its most basic form, you take your holiday in the home of someone who lives in a completely different part of the country (near the sea for example, if you do not) and you reciprocate by letting that family use your home during the same period. Both families get to experience a part of the country that is new to them and the holiday costs very little more than the gas money required to travel to your destination. Other benefits to a house swap, is that your home is not left unattended while you are away and (depending on the folk who are going to stay there) you will have someone to take care of pets and plants, which will be yet another saving (you don't need to pay to kennel pets or to get a house sitter in to water plants).

Another huge advantage of house swapping is that if you link up with an overseas family, you could experience a foreign country, although travel cost might make such a vacation unaffordable. It is however a thought to put on the back burner for when your finances improve.

Vehicle purchases: The chances are that you will not easily be looking to purchase an automobile if you have been laid off or during a particularly difficult financial period, such as a recession. However, should you find yourself in the car market for whatever reason, make sure to really shop around first. Many dealers will be prepared to offer better deals on models that are (very) soon to be replaced by a newer version. You can also consider purchasing a used vehicle, although with such a purchase you need to do your homework to ensure that the automobile is in the (working) condition that the owner claims it to be in.

Make an effort to save: This suggestion may sound somewhat strange if you have been retrenched or are living through a recession, but even if you put 1% to 5% of the income that you have generated within the month, into your savings account, this small amount will slowly build up. You should not miss this amount each month and at a future point, should you have an out of the ordinary expense, you will have some money to cover it. It is normally when we can least afford to pay anything "extra", that a family member or much-loved pet falls ill, or the automobile gives problems.

Continue your payments: This may sound like another strange suggestion, but once you have paid off an account, continue to "write a cheque" for the same amount (or even for 50% of the original amount) and deposit this money into your savings account. The reason behind this thinking is that you have managed to live during the period that you were paying this particular account, so keep at it in order to build up an amount of money for emergencies.

Credit cards: It is all too easy to pay for a purchase using a credit card. The reality that you are spending money (often money that you can ill afford to spend) does not really hit home when you pass a piece of plastic to the teller. Counting out the hard cash and handing it over, makes the transaction and more importantly, the money that you have spent, more real. The same applies to writing out a cheque as well, so wherever possible, use your credit card only when you are travelling or when you require a receipt for tax purposes.

The best advice that you can get regarding your credit card (except from possibly cutting it up), is to always pay the full amount that you owe at the end of each month. Each time you pay only the minimum amount, the sum that remains will continue to accrue interest to the point that you may ultimately end up paying many times more than the original selling price of the item.

Tax: It often pays to take advice from a tax consultant, even if you are experiencing difficult financial times. Although you will be paying for this advice, a consultant will show you how to look out for each legal tax deduction that you are entitled to and through this approach, you will end up paying less on your tax return.

Understand the potential problems of a "dual earning family": Most people would be absolutely thrilled at the thought of having two salaries come into the home each month but be aware that there are many "unseen" financial pitfalls to having both partners earning. Statistics from the US Labor Department indicates that in families where both partners are working, between half and two thirds of the second salary is spent on items that would not have featured if the family was receiving a single pay check.

- **Domestic help** – When only one partner is earning, the other invariably remains at home and attends to household duties such as cooking, cleaning, washing and ironing. If the second partner enters the work force, time to run the home becomes limited and domestic help, at a price, is invariably sought.
- **Child care** – Working mothers are no longer able to take care of their children and normally seek out a day care centre for the youngsters (age dependant). Such centre cost money, including the often "unseen" extra costs of gas, which would not have been spent if the children had remained at home under their mother's supervision.
- **Labor – saving luxuries** – Dry cleaning and take out meals are often high on the list of working families. Both are expensive, and both become a regular expense in such families. When

both partners are working, the family often function under the misconception that there is a lot more money coming in and that they are justified in spending in a way that they would certainly not do if only one partner was earning.

- **Transport costs** – Although in select cases, both partners will work at the same place, this does not always happen and sometimes, even if they do, they may be on different shifts, which necessitates that each still uses their own vehicle. With two automobiles on the road, the cost of gas doubles, as does the so called "unseen" expenses, such as wear and tear on tires and all related vehicle "running" costs.

- **Double wardrobes**: When both partners are earning, both will need to be dressed for the positions that they hold. Even if both partners do not have managerial or senior positions, administrative staff, secretaries and "front desk" staff are required to dress smartly, and this costs money.

- **Taxation**: Two career households are going to be taxed accordingly, which at the end of the day, means less money in you pocket. The shocking truth regarding a middle – class duel earning family, is that they will have earned (put in their pockets) less than 20% more money than if only one partner was working.

CHAPTER 22

Develop the correct mind set

When we are working for a company, many of the day to day decisions are taken on our behalf by other people. Most people tend to specialise in a career of some or other description and once they are established in an organisation, they concentrate specifically on their job. In other words, a mechanic will spend his working day stripping down and repairing the engines of vehicles that have been brought into his specific garage. His supervisor and the owner of the business, will expect little more from the mechanic, than that the person does a great job of repairing automobiles. In fact, many organisations encourage their staff to focus on and become expert in the line of work that they were hired to perform. In most instances, the mechanic will not be expected to be available at reception to deal with customers, nor will he have the challenges and headaches of having to balance the company's books. Other people, who are not expected to fix car engines, will be responsible for those tasks. And at the end of each week or month, the mechanic and all other staff will receive their pay, regardless if they have been ill during that period or on leave and even though each person has concentrated only on their job and not had to worry about the "bigger picture".

So, what on earth does any of this have to do with being laid off, or looking for ways to make extra income during difficult financial times?

While you still worked at a company and concentrated on your specific job, the organization most likely had marketing staff, who brought business (money) into the company, and public relations staff, who were the company's "front window", showing it off to its best advantage and bookkeepers / accountants who ensured that the money was correctly invested.

Once you are on your own, you need to market yourself and do your own public relations and make sure that you are working with and investing (or at least, not wasting) the money that you are working so hard to generate. In many ways, you need to reinvent yourself. You need a new mindset, a new way of "looking at" the world and what it can offer.

Develop a winning attitude: If you have been retrenched or even if you are still holding down a job, but realise that you need to generate extra income, you will need to broaden your "mental approach" to life. For the person who has been laid off, there is no longer a "big daddy" looking after you. In many cases, your company would have contributed towards a medical and retirement plan for you and you may even have received a 13TH cheque (or bonus) and a housing subsidy. None of this applies if you have been retrenched and you will need to develop a "winning attitude" to ensure that you and yours will survive the "harder" times that lie ahead.

Robert Reich, America's 22nd Secretary of Labor is quoted as saying: *"In the new economy, with unpredictable earning, two tracts are emerging, the fast track and the slow track and the absence of gradations between"*. If you are going to survive the difficult financial time that lie ahead, you need to get onto the "fast track".

- **Change your reality** - People resist change through fear of the unknown, a lack of understanding that change can be beneficial, laziness and who knows what else. Most Folks prefer to remain as they are rather than attempt to change their circumstances. By that I mean that people find ways to live with their circumstances rather than source ways to drastically improve their situation. Believe it or not, the quickest way to begin making money is to change your way of thinking. The concept that if you are productive and honest after signing on with a company, you will have a job for life and will receive a pension to take care of your financial needs after retirement is no longer valid.

- **Choose to be wealthy**: It is a universal reality that most of the truly wealthy people today, are not necessarily well educated or talented. They became rich because they chose to become so. These people did not believe that they had limitations, to them nothing was impossible.

- **Do not be put off by your own perceptions**: Obtaining good grades at school has benefited some, but good grades are not necessarily a prerequisite to financial stability or success. What most people don't realise is that school teaches us (known) facts. The better we are at remembering these facts, the better we do at school. Conventionally cleaver folk, land careers on their (school / university) qualifications, which represents achievements from their past, whereas most highly successful people, are making money due to their present (and future) need to achieve progressively more and more.

Remember that you no longer have a "big daddy" once you have been retrenched. Do not be limited by your perceptions of what you can achieve. Set realistic goals and strive daily to achieve them. You may find that you become not only financially stable, but wealthy beyond your expectations.

Good luck with whatever project you attempt.

Best wishes
Marc-Charles Nicolas

CPSIA information can be obtained
at www.ICGtesting.com
Printed in the USA
BVHW030046311220
596783BV00001B/8